THE
ENTREPRENEURIAL
EDGE

REAL FOUNDERS TELL THE STORIES BEHIND BUSINESSES THAT ENDURE

FEATURING VISIONARY ENTREPRENEURS

PASSIONPRENEUR®
PUBLISHING

Publishing information
Publishing and design facilitated by
Passionpreneur Publishing
A division of Passionpreneur Organization Pty Ltd
ABN: 48640637529

Melbourne, VIC | Australia
www.passionpreneurpublishing.com

Dedication

*To those who dare to create,
persevere, and lead with heart.
May these stories remind you
that every great venture
begins with belief...and
ends with conviction.*

*And to all those who—visibly
and invisibly—support them.*

Table of Contents

Acknowledgements

This book would not have been possible without, first and foremost, the entrepreneurs who decided to back themselves. Not only in launching, growing and sustaining businesses, but in believing that their stories and voices were worthy of attention.

Thank you to the literary agents, publishing team and content reviewers who made this book possible.

Life is a storm, my young friend. You will bask in the sunlight one moment, be shattered on the rocks the next. What makes you a man is what you do when that storm comes.

— The Count of Monte Cristo

Introduction

Entrepreneurship is often described in terms of strategy, scale, and success. But behind every business worth building is something deeper: a human story shaped by belief, pressure, risk, instinct, and resilience. That is what this book is really about—twenty-eight entrepreneurs, each bringing a distinct voice, a hard-won perspective, and a lesson learned through experience.

These stories reveal that entrepreneurship is not a straight line from idea to outcome. Instead, it is a series of decisions made in uncertainty, often with limited resources, constant change, and no guarantee of approval. What unites these contributors is not that they all took the same path, but that they all chose to move forward anyway.

You will find practical wisdom here, but also something less easy to measure: conviction. Some chapters speak to leadership, others to innovation, relationships, systems, or reinvention, yet each one reflects the same truth: business is built by people, and people are driven by purpose as much as profit.

This collection is an invitation to think more clearly, act more boldly, and build more intentionally. As you read, I hope you do not only see what these entrepreneurs created, but also what they overcame, what they learned, and what they would do again. Their stories may begin in different places, but together they point to one powerful idea: the future belongs to those willing to create it.

— Omar Hamdi
Founder & CEO, Pathos Communications plc
London, 2026

Pathos Communications is a London-listed media technology company (LSE: NEWS) and the fastest-growing advertising/ marketing firm in Europe according to the Financial Times FT1000.

CHAPTER 1

The Entrepreneur's Guide to Thinking With AI

By Amelia Castellanos,
Founder, Buffaloe Digital

I've spent the majority of my career at the crossover of brand, commerce, and change. Today, through Buffaloe Digital, I help consumer brands modernize how they sell, communicate, and scale. With a background rooted in journalism and marketing, I focus on examining evidence and identifying patterns. Most importantly, I need to know why something *works*.

Although the data has always existed in e-commerce, until recently it has been buried within various platforms, fragmented dashboards, and disconnected systems. As a result, entrepreneurs and the brands they're building often make decisions based on assumptions instead of genuine insight, a hastiness which often leads them astray. I initially became interested in artificial intelligence because it offers something businesses have struggled with for years: the ability to ask the right questions and—finally—get clear answers.

When I discuss AI with clients, one of the biggest misconceptions is that it will replace human jobs or turn their business into something mechanical, lifeless, and sterile. But in reality, the opposite tends to happen.

When implemented properly, AI helps brands become more *human*. It allows teams to understand customers more clearly, communicate more effectively, and respond to behavior in real time rather than relying on guesswork.

For entrepreneurs to get this right, they have to be capable of utilizing the technology judiciously. Offering far more than simple AI tools, modern platforms give brands more flexibility to define the tone and identity first. Once those parameters are established, the technology operates within them. Rather than sounding generic, the output begins to reflect the brand voice. No longer on autopilot, the AI becomes a genuinely collaborative force.

Even so, the rapid proliferation of AI tools and platforms can feel overwhelming, especially for entrepreneurs just starting out or brands still finding their footing. With this challenge in mind, here are two areas you can focus on to deliver immediate value:

1. **On-site experience.** This includes all events that are triggered when a customer browses your website:

merchandising, product recommendations, personalization, and search. These elements determine whether someone quickly finds what they want or leaves frustrated.

2. **Off-site experience**. The channels a brand controls outside the website itself, including CRM systems, email marketing, and SMS messaging. These outlets drive retention, repeat purchases, and extended relationships with the company.

These two environments are mutually dependent: a strong website experience without ongoing communication limits growth, while strong communication without relevant on-site content wastes potential opportunities. As the brands that are experiencing the highest levels of growth realize, AI's power lies in connecting both sides of the user experience, allowing each to inform the other.

For years, businesses, whether large enterprises or startups, have been trying to understand their customers by blindly navigating through a maze of data. Like the 'X' on a treasure map, AI takes the guesswork out of that process by connecting information across disparate systems, highlighting patterns that might otherwise have been missed.

With AI's assistance, entrepreneurs can finally get answers to the questions they've been asking for decades. Who are our customers today? What are they buying, when are they buying it, and what are they searching for that we are failing to highlight?

Even though these questions directly affect the bottom line, many businesses struggle to answer them clearly. The uncomfortable truth is this: some brands consistently target the wrong customers. As your business scales, there's a good chance you'll outgrow your original audience without realizing it. In the process, you could easily waste time and resources speaking to a customer who no longer exists.

In today's world, AI allows you to recognize that shift, sometimes even before it happens. The value of AI lies not just in the insights it generates but also in its ability to accelerate what comes next.

Instead of creating reports destined to sit in unused dashboards, AI can help teams identify specific actions to execute in response to the data. It can also highlight which products to promote, which audiences respond to certain messaging, and where marketing investments should be focused. It can even help entrepreneurs and their organizations move faster from information-gathering to implementation.

There is a caveat, however: AI is only as effective as the information it receives. Human teams must provide accurate data, ask meaningful questions, and evaluate the results carefully.

In one of the more interesting outcomes I've seen, AI encourages people to think more critically about their work. Used well, it pushes teams to challenge assumptions and scrutinize data more carefully, allowing for better questions and more deliberate decision-making.

I often compare this to geometry class. Some students produce the right answer but struggle to explain how they reached it, which is why teachers always want to see the steps. AI is similar. It might generate an answer quickly, but teams still need to understand the reasoning behind it. It is that process that strengthens analytical thinking across the organization.

This is what I mean when I say that AI, done properly, does not replace human expertise but sharpens it.

For entrepreneurs beginning to integrate AI into their business, here are a few practical steps.

First, start with a clear business question. Rather than implementing technology for its own sake, identify the problems that need solving and allow AI to analyze them.

Second, ensure your foundational data is organized and reliable. If product data or tracking is inconsistent, AI is incapable of generating meaningful insights.

Third, create connectivity between the on-site and off-site experiences. Customer behavior on your website should inform all messages they receive through email, SMS, or other channels.

Fourth, treat AI as a collaborator. Encourage teams to experiment while maintaining responsibility for final decisions.

And finally, cultivate curiosity. The more thoughtful the questions, the more valuable the answers become.

At its core, AI offers something entrepreneurs have been seeking for years: clarity and accurate optics. But its true advantage emerges when a thoughtful team uses AI to ask smarter questions, test better activations, and respond more effectively.

The technology is not here to replace the human side of business, but to amplify it. And for entrepreneurs in today's world looking to scale, that crucial partnership between human insight and AI may create the very advantage your business has been lacking.

CHAPTER 2

When the Market Talks, Listen

By Cody Spears,
Owner, TraceMySpace and Author,
Lead Big Book Series

I've met a lot of entrepreneurs who are brilliant on day one, then exhausted by month six.

They launch something, give it a solid run...only to abandon it and jump to the next idea when results aren't fast enough. From the outside looking in, it's frustrating because you can see the potential. Sometimes the product is good, as well as the marketing. At other times, they simply lack the patience to allow the product to come to fruition.

If I've learned anything about building businesses from the ground up, it's this: consistency pays off more than quick results. If you believe in something enough to keep showing up for it, and maintain a steady presence long enough for the market to actually respond, you give yourself the chance to earn something most people never do: momentum.

When I took over TraceMySpace, it was a concept rather than a proven market solution. While it was promising technology with high potential, it had not yet been fully validated by real-world demand. Because I knew that going in, I wasn't looking for a home run in the first inning. I was playing the long game.

Taking this strategic perspective requires something many entrepreneurs don't like to practice: the willingness to adapt your plan in response to what's actually happening, not what you *hoped* would happen.

Here's the reality. You can walk into entrepreneurship with a clear picture of what you are building, who it is for, and how it is going to grow. You can have the best plan in the world...

Until the market starts talking back.

When you stop treating feedback as noise and start treating it as actionable data, customer-led innovation is the result. By paying close enough attention to this valuable commodity, you can start to let the market refine your product, your positioning, and sometimes even your entire business model.

This does not mean becoming a "yes man," or chasing every request—but it *does* mean staying alert to opportunity, especially when it shows up in places you did not anticipate.

I've watched entrepreneurs miss opportunities because they were fixated on a linear journey. Being committed to their original plan above all else, they couldn't see the value sitting right in front of them. Sometimes, that opportunity is far from glamorous. Sometimes, it's as simple as a customer saying: "Have you ever thought about using it this way?" If your ego's so tied to being right that you cannot hear that question, you miss far more than feedback. You miss *direction*.

I can say this with confidence, because it's exactly how we have grown. We spend very little on marketing, because satisfied customers are our most efficient marketing tool. Word travels quickly when the product is right and the experience is consistent.

I push that with our team all the time. It's not only about putting out a product, but also about ensuring that everything we release feels perfect. Because once it is in the world, it represents us.

Let me share a practical example of how customer-led innovation becomes visible in the real world. Some of our customers reach out to us with the intention of outfitting an entire facility. Big numbers, big orders. Sometimes they're ready to buy 50 toolboxes' worth of inserts on day one.

We could take the quick win and accept the full order immediately. But that is not how you build trust, and it is not how you build long-term growth either.

So I tell them to start with one. Order inserts for just one toolbox first. See it. Touch it. Use it in your environment. Because I'm confident in what we do, I would much rather earn their trust than prematurely force a big sale.

Of course, that approach almost always leads to the bigger order—but now it is anchored in trust.

If you are an entrepreneur, that should tell you something. If you are always chasing the fastest transaction, you may be sacrificing the hard-won loyalty that actually builds a business over the long term.

Practicing customer-led innovation also gives you access to a steady stream of ideas.

In the aerospace industry, for example, customers will often call and ask: "What if you did this?" or "What if you added that?" And while we have already tested (or are currently working on) some of these ideas, others we never would have considered on our own.

This is where many entrepreneurs get confused. Listening is important, but it does not mean surrendering your standards.

I had a customer recently tell me that our inserts were "too perfect." He wanted general shapes instead of precise cutouts; in other words, a simplified version of what we pride ourselves on. I understood what he wanted, but I also understood what it would do. If we intentionally produce something which does not meet our standards of excellence, we weaken the brand we have fought so hard to build.

So I told him the truth. Although we are open to feedback and receptive to new ideas, we will not do anything that harms our brand.

That is the line. Ego has nothing to do with it.

For what it's worth, ego is not always a negative thing. You need a certain level of confidence to build anything. But the ego becomes dangerous when it becomes a blindfold.

One thing I tell the people around me is this: if I am not good at something, tell me. If you see a better way, speak up.

This is a cultural choice, a leadership choice. Ultimately, it is a business choice. Because if you insist on being the only voice in the room, you may feel powerful, but you are limiting your growth.

Customer-led innovation starts with humility, admitting you do not have all the answers, and then building a system that lets answers find you.

That is how you let the market rewrite your plan without losing yourself or your standards in the process.

CHAPTER 3

The Corporate Lessons Startups Ignore

By Dr. Cordell Robinson,
Founder and CEO,
Brownstone Consulting Firm

I am a U.S. Navy veteran and the CEO and founder of Brownstone Consulting Firm, a cybersecurity and program support services company. I am also the founder of Shaping Futures Foundation, a nonprofit dedicated to expanding educational opportunities for youth in East Africa. My career has taken me from military service to corporate environments and eventually into entrepreneurship, where I now operate across cybersecurity, business operations, and international development. Moving between those worlds has taught me something that runs against much of the mythology surrounding startup culture.

Scrappy startups have a lot to learn from polished corporates.

In startup culture, large corporations are often portrayed as slow, bureaucratic, and resistant to change. Startups are celebrated for speed and flexibility, as well as their willingness to break rules. But after working inside large organizations and then building my own company, I've come to see that the best founders don't reject corporate discipline—they adapt it.

The systems that help large companies scale, retain talent, and manage risk are often the same ones startups eventually need to scale effectively. From my perspective, the most valuable lessons fall into three areas: process, people, and compliance.

The importance of process is one of the most crucial lessons I carried from corporate life into entrepreneurship. Startups often pride themselves on operating without structure. In the early stages, that can work: everyone doing a little bit of everything, decisions taken quickly, the company moving forward by momentum alone. But that only works for so long. Without clear direction for you as the founder or CEO, there is no structure for anyone else.

Process creates clarity. It establishes expectations, defines responsibilities, and allows teams to operate without constant oversight. Without strong processes, the organization depends entirely on individual memory and improvisation, which becomes unsustainable as it grows.

I've seen how large organizations build baseline processes that allow them to operate at scale while still adapting to local realities. The culture in one place can look different to that in another, and a third location might operate differently again. Yet across those environments the core systems remain consistent. Understanding that balance matters for entrepreneurs. Processes should enhance agility, and they should create the foundation that makes growth possible.

The second lesson is about people.

Corporate organizations understand people. They also understand something that many startups underestimate: retention is emotional. Employees want to feel valued and connected to the organization they work for.

Large companies often build this connection through recognition and small but meaningful incentives. Bonuses, benefits, milestone awards, and simple gestures of appreciation help reinforce the idea that employees matter.

These things might seem minor, but they are not. They create loyalty.

Startups sometimes assume that the primary motivation for employees is the promise of equity or the possibility of a major financial exit. But not everyone wants to be an entrepreneur. Running a business requires enormous energy and risk tolerance. Many talented professionals simply want meaningful work, clear direction, and a stable environment where their contributions are recognized.

One of the best examples of retention I've seen came from a small business rather than a corporation. My dentist, now retired, used to shut down his entire practice once a year and take his office somewhere nice. The result was loyalty rarely seen elsewhere. I started going to that dental office in 2002, and many of the same employees were still there more than twenty years later.

Startups don't need corporate budgets to build loyalty like that, but they do need intention. Recognition, a sense of community, shared milestones: these things can transform a group of employees into a team that genuinely believes in the mission.

The third lesson is compliance.

For many founders, compliance sounds like bureaucracy. In reality, though, compliance is the framework keeping organizations safe as they grow. It is compliance that establishes the policies and standards guiding behavior across the organization. These policies ensure the business operates legally, protects its assets, and creates consistent expectations for employees and clients.

Cybersecurity, my area of expertise, sits underneath the umbrella of compliance. Because without a culture of compliance, cybersecurity tools alone cannot protect your business. If employees ignore policies or mishandle sensitive information, even the best security systems become ineffective. Technology cannot compensate for behavior.

Small companies often think they are too insignificant to attract attention from bad actors. They believe that the bigger the organization, the bigger the target. In practice, what cybercriminals have realized is that smaller organizations are often more vulnerable precisely because they lack the guardrails that larger companies have developed over time.

The lesson here is broader than cybersecurity. Well-designed compliance structures are an organization's safeguard against risk, whether it's financial, operational, or reputational. Building a compliance culture early is far easier than trying to impose one later. Waiting until you have hundreds of employees before establishing clear policies makes changing procedures that much more difficult.

Entrepreneurs should protect the speed and creativity that make them powerful. But founders should also recognize that corporate environments have spent decades refining systems that support scale. A good startup, after all, is one built to scale.

The most effective companies combine both worlds, remaining entrepreneurial in mindset while borrowing the operational discipline that allows organizations to scale. Process provides structure, the people create loyalty, and compliance protects the business.

And all of it must be anchored in a clear mission.

This is where corporations excel. They are skilled at tapping into emotion and helping employees feel connected to a larger purpose. Startups should do the same. Don't assume people are going to believe in your mission because it's new. You have to make them believe, and if you can do that they will become invested in the company's success.

Scrappy energy can start companies, but discipline and structure are what enable them to become enduring institutions.

CHAPTER 4

Success Is Maintained, Not Achieved

By Cristina Busu, MS, BCBA,
Founder, Help Hope Solutions

When I started Help Hope Solutions, I didn't have a vision board with a revenue target or a specific number of employees in mind. I didn't wake up one day thinking that once I hit a specific milestone, then I would finally be successful.

I started with a much simpler goal: to help as many children as possible.

Help Hope Solutions was built to support parents seeking ABA therapy for children with autism and other learning or behavioral challenges. From the beginning, the need was overwhelming.

There are always more families searching for support, more children waiting for services, more gaps to fill. That reality, that there is always another child or family that needs help, has shaped the way I think about success.

For me, success has never been a finish line. It has always been a responsibility.

Many entrepreneurs imagine a defining moment. A revenue figure, a team size, a specific office building. A milestone that signals that you've made it. But what I've learned over time is that success doesn't arrive like that. It builds gradually, and once it builds, it demands maintenance. Success, and the maintenance of that success, are the same outcome.

Early on, growth felt straightforward. Open one clinic, serve more children. Expand, then expand again. Hire more staff, reach more families. But growth quickly exposes limitations. At some point, expansion becomes about being able to effectively train staff, navigate regulatory complexity, and manage culture.

I could have outsourced many of those components. In some cases, that's what I did. But when something didn't feel right, I had to pull it back in-house. I learned that I cannot lead what I do not understand. Even if I delegate, I must know enough to recognize when something is off. When you view success as an ongoing process, that level of visibility is crucial.

One of the biggest misconceptions about entrepreneurship is that once you reach a certain level, you can relax. That the hardest work is now behind you. In reality, maintaining success introduces a different kind of work. It may be less chaotic, but it requires more precision.

Think of business like a puzzle. Every department, every role, every process is a piece. When those pieces interlock properly, the picture works. But if you pull one piece out and replace it without considering how it connects to the others, you risk disrupting the entire structure.

Many entrepreneurs drive their companies in the direction of their strengths. Some are people-focused, like me. Others are financially driven, while others are obsessed with systems or technology. That's natural. But maintenance requires seeing the entire puzzle clearly. If you overcorrect in one area without understanding its impact on the rest, you can destabilize what you worked so hard to build in the first place.

Consequently, each innovation must be approached carefully. For example, I've seen tools that promise dramatic increases in efficiency or productivity. On paper, they look transformative. But if implementing them disrupts morale, culture, or workflow to the point of instability, the cost may outweigh the benefit. Growth of this kind, growth that fractures the foundation, is not true growth. It is erosion.

Over time, maintenance may also require adjusting to generational shifts. What motivated my team 10 years ago is not what motivates them today. In my experience, Millennials want visible progression and affirmation of impact, while Gen Z wants clarity of purpose and alignment with their personal lives.

If I had stayed attached to the leadership strategies that worked a decade ago, we would have stagnated. Maintaining success means staying grounded in reality. It means listening. It means observing people, even when they cannot articulate exactly what they need. Culture is not static; it evolves. If leadership does not evolve with it, success will slowly deteriorate.

There is another aspect of maintenance that entrepreneurs often ignore: self-maintenance.

Trust me when I say entrepreneurship is not a five-year sprint, although I know it can feel like it. If you assume there will be a point where you can finally exhale and catch your breath, you will burn out chasing it. I have reached many milestones as the company has expanded and built teams. Yet none of those moments eliminated the need to keep building.

I have had to accept that my role is to continuously set standards; to adjust, refine, and protect the integrity of what we've built while staying open to what it can become.

Rather than a single benchmark or accolade, I measure success by how many children we can help. But that's me. What has worked so well for me and my business may not work for someone else. Even so, I do believe this: if you treat success as a destination, you risk losing it. If you treat it as something living, requiring ongoing care, recalibration, and humility, you are far more likely to sustain it.

Maintenance, then, is strategic. It is the discipline of seeing clearly, adapting carefully, and leading consciously.

In my experience, that discipline is exactly what separates temporary wins from enduring impact.

CHAPTER 5

Winning From Within:
The Insurgent Advantage

By Gary Preisser,
Co-Founder, Stonebriar Wealth Advisors

When markets become uncertain, industries tend to consolidate. Capital concentrates. Compliance tightens. Large institutions become even more protective of their systems. In times like these, many entrepreneurs assume that scale is safety and that competing against established players is a losing battle.

I've come to believe the opposite.

In entrepreneurship, incumbents are the established players. They dominate market share, control infrastructure, and operate within deeply embedded systems. Entrepreneurs, by contrast, are insurgents. They are challengers. Smaller, more flexible, less constrained by legacy processes. Incumbents optimize for stability and protection, insurgents for agility and alignment. In stable markets, incumbents often win on scale. In changing markets, insurgents often win on adaptability.

I worked inside the traditional financial system before launching Stonebriar Wealth Advisors, giving me a unique perspective on how large firms operate. They are not malicious, I realized, but structured. They are engineered for scale, litigation, protection, and operational efficiency. The challenge is that optimizing for scale often sacrifices proximity, and losing proximity can cost you alignment with the individual client.

That is the insurgent's opening.

In my industry, many firms begin by asking the same questions. How much do you have? How old are you? How do you feel about risk? Clients are categorized into templates and slotted into portfolios that look nearly identical to thousands of others with similar "profiles". The focus is almost always on average rates of return; it is never on actual performance or integration. It's clean, it's compliant. But it's not personal.

Successful entrepreneurship requires better questions. In finance, it's less about asking a client how much money they have and more about asking them what that money is really for. The purpose changes the calculus.

When you begin with purpose, you naturally uncover timing. When will these assets be used? What income will be required? What obligations must be met? Once you understand timing, decisions become clearer. Risk, often an emotional label, becomes a function of when capital must perform.

Regardless of industry, this simple shift can be difficult for large institutions to execute. Integration at scale is expensive, and coordination requires more than a product shelf. It requires conversation, which does not scale as easily as standardized portfolios.

This is where insurgents gain ground.

By building my business around integration, strategy is coordinated across accounts, time horizons, and client stages. It is bespoke by design.

Some of the pushback I get from the industry goes something like this: while the approach might be thoughtful, it is not scalable. This is wrong. When you ask the right questions, the process becomes more efficient. As an entrepreneur, as an insurgent, you often don't need to rebuild the entire system. Instead, you can leverage the architecture incumbents have already created.

Instead of taking custody of client assets ourselves, for example, we use established institutions to hold them. The infrastructure of the financial industry provides safety and the operational backbone. What we control is the advisory layer, which includes the strategy and the integration. This powerful hybrid model allows clients to feel secure within a familiar system while benefiting from tailored, integrated advice. By doing so, it allows smaller firms to outperform expectations without taking on unnecessary structural risk.

The same thinking applies to any industry. Think of software. Many successful startups build on top of existing platforms, using cloud services, payment processors, and open-source tools created by incumbents. Instead of competing at the infrastructure layer, they compete at the intelligence and user-experience layer. They leverage scale while preserving flexibility.

As a co-founder, starting from scratch in a new market over four years, we grew to approximately $400 million in assets under management through education and client referrals. We prioritized purpose and clarity, for ourselves and our clients. Because when people understand how their capital aligns with their life, they respond.

The broader lesson here extends beyond wealth management.

In any mature industry, incumbents optimize for compliance and predictability. They must, because public shareholders, regulators, and internal governance demand it. But that same optimization creates blind spots by reducing flexibility and discouraging internal critique. In the process, it can choke innovation.

Not burdened by those constraints, insurgents can challenge assumptions and integrate services others keep separate. They can democratize knowledge that large organizations prefer to keep opaque. Most importantly, they can stay close to the customer.

Changing market dynamics amplify this advantage, regardless of industry. When markets shift, regulations evolve, or consumer expectations rise, clients crave clarity. They want someone who understands their specific situation, not to be assigned to a category.

As I understand it, this is what will set your business apart: being closer to the client, to the purpose, and to the friction points larger organizations often overlook. This is usually framed as disruption, but there's more to it than that. Entrepreneurs should recognize that scale without alignment becomes brittle. They should strive to build systems that grow without losing intimacy.

Increasingly, business success will belong to those who understand how to work within and take advantage of existing structures, while maintaining the ability to think and operate independently of them—all while keeping the client's individual needs as the priority.

This is the insurgent advantage. And in a world that promises nothing but change, it may be the most durable advantage out there.

CHAPTER 6

In Business, Relationships Still Win

By Geri Lynn,
Founder and Owner, Geri Lynn Nissan

I have spent most of my career in the automotive business, an industry many people assume revolves around numbers, negotiations, and closing deals. From the outside, it often appears purely transactional. A customer walks in, a salesperson walks to a manager whom the customer never has the "honor" of meeting, the salesperson returns to the customer and presents them with options, a price is negotiated, and the customer drives away. That is the version of the business many people expect.

But that has never been how I have experienced it.

For me, running a dealership has always been about people first. Cars are simply the reason they walk through the door. What really determines whether someone returns, recommends you, or trusts you with one of the largest purchases of their life is how they feel while they are with you.

Over the years, I have come to believe something that runs against much of the traditional advice entrepreneurs hear. The strongest advantage a business can build is not its technology, pricing strategy, or product differentiation: it is the relationships it forms with the people around it.

And those relationships start inside the organization.

If you have ever run a business, you have probably heard the advice that leaders must separate emotion from leadership. The idea is that professionalism requires *distance*. The leader must be objective, disciplined, and detached. Emotion, according to this view, only clouds judgment. At first glance, that advice sounds reasonable. But in my experience, it misses something essential about how businesses can go from simply operating to thriving.

When leaders remove the emotional side of leadership, work-places become transactional. People show up, do their assigned tasks, and go home. The organization might still function, but it rarely becomes something meaningful to the people inside it. It becomes a job rather than a shared mission. I believe the real issue is how we misunderstand emotion.

Leadership does not mean abandoning accountability or struc-ture. It means recognizing that people are human beings first and employees second. When we lead with that understanding, something shifts. The workplace becomes a place where people feel valued, supported, and connected to something larger than their individual roles.

That does not mean leaders avoid difficult decisions. I have had moments where I had to let long-time team members go. Those are never easy decisions, especially when you have invested time, patience, and effort into helping someone succeed.

But accountability and care are not opposites.

In many ways, I think leadership resembles parenting more than management theory. When we raise our children, we hold them accountable. We correct them. Sometimes we discipline them. Yet we never withdraw the emotional foundation of the relationship. We do not stop caring about them simply because they made a mistake.

In business, the same principle can apply. You can expect excellence from your team while still treating them with empathy and respect. When people know that their leader genuinely cares about them, they are more likely to rise to those expectations. Sometimes they even surprise you.

I have watched employees grow into roles they never imagined possible because someone believed in them long enough for them to believe in themselves. When that culture takes hold, values become shared rather than enforced, and the workplace becomes a lived culture that ultimately shapes how customers experience the business.

People often ask whether a relationship-driven approach actually translates into measurable results. In other words, does it sell cars?

In my experience, the answer is yes—and often in ways that are more powerful than traditional marketing strategies.

One of my favorite examples happened recently with a young customer who came to purchase a vehicle. During our conversation, he mentioned that his grandfather had bought cars from our dealership years ago. His father had also purchased several vehicles from us over the years, and now he had been sent to us as well. Three generations of the same family had walked through our doors. This customer walked away with more than a car: we sent him away with three bottles of wine and a thank-you note, one for each generation.

And we walked away with more than a sale: we received the kind of loyalty that only comes from relationships developed over time. When someone trusts you enough to recommend your business to their children and grandchildren, it means something deeper has taken place.

It means they felt seen.

That idea matters more than many entrepreneurs realize. When customers enter a business, they want to know that they matter as people, not just as transactions. Sometimes that means helping someone even when they cannot buy from you yet.

I once had a customer come into the dealership who was in a difficult financial situation. She could not purchase a vehicle at that time. Instead of simply sending her away, I gave her my card and cell phone number and told her to keep in touch. I told her that her situation would change eventually and that she should call me when it did. Even if she walked out without a car, I wanted her to leave feeling like she mattered. Moments like that shape how people remember your business.

Trust also plays a larger role than many entrepreneurs appreciate. When someone purchases a vehicle, they are handing over deeply personal information: their identification, financial details, and credit history. In many ways, they are placing their identity in your hands.

Entrepreneurship is often framed as a relentless pursuit of success, with founders encouraged to chase growth, market share, and competitive advantage. But over the years, I have come to believe that success often arrives as a byproduct of something else.

When businesses focus on taking care of people, employees, customers, and partners alike, they create environments where trust and loyalty can grow. Those relationships become the foundation upon which everything else is built. You can chase success directly, or you can focus on building something meaningful for the people around you.

In my experience, the second path often leads to the first.

So if there is one step I would encourage entrepreneurs to take, it is this: look closely at the way people feel when they interact with your business. Not just your customers, but your team as well.

Ask yourself whether your workplace feels transactional or relational. Ask whether people feel seen, heard, and respected when they walk through the door. Because even though products evolve, technology advances, and markets shift in changing times, the human need for trust, connection, and respect remains remarkably constant.

Businesses that understand that truth often build something far more durable than a successful company. They build meaning for your brand, your team, and everyone who walks through the door.

Loyalty that lasts for generations simply becomes the reward.

CHAPTER 7

The Business of Being Real

By Julianna Doherty,
CEO, Recycle Away

I used to think authenticity was something you either had or you didn't.

You hear it all the time in entrepreneurship: be authentic, stay true to yourself, build a brand people believe in. It sounds right, and it sounds simple, but I think it's completely misunderstood. What I've learned over time is that authenticity is not a personality trait, a tone of voice, or something you layer onto a business once it already exists. It's a discipline. If you don't build it into the foundation of what you're creating, people will feel that disconnect long before they can articulate it.

Early in my career, I had an advantage I didn't fully appreciate at the time. My first business was built around a customer I understood firsthand, because I was living that reality myself.

I was a mom with four young kids, trying to get through the day without dropping the ball somewhere. The product, the messaging, the chaos behind it, it was all real because I was living it in real time. There was no gap between the brand and the experience. At one point, my phone number was on the back of the packaging, and a buyer from a major grocery chain called, expecting customer service, and got me in the car with my kids instead. That moment did not hurt the business. If anything, it helped it, because it was real, and real builds trust faster than anything else.

But the lesson isn't that you should only build for customers who are exactly like you. That would be far too limiting, and it would miss the real point. You do not have to be the customer, but your business has to be built in a way that is authentic to the customer. There is a difference.

I have seen founders identify a perfect gap in the market. The data supports it, the timing looks right, and the margins make sense. They build something that technically works, yet it never really connects. Usually, that happens because it was built from analysis rather than understanding.

If you are not the customer, then you have to bring the customer into the business in a real way. Not as a theoretical end user, but as a voice that shapes decisions. As a presence that influences how the product is built, how it is sold, and how it shows up in the world.

This becomes especially obvious when you think about who represents the business.

If you are building a product for parents, a polished salesperson who understands retail strategy better than real life may get you into the room, but they will not necessarily build trust. Put a pediatrician in that conversation, or a parent who lives the problem every day, and everything changes. The message lands differently. The questions get sharper. The connection becomes immediate. That is not branding in the shallow sense. That is authenticity built into the system.

The same principle applies internally. Entrepreneurship often rewards the idea of hiring the "best" people on paper, the ones with the strongest resumes or the most obvious credentials. Sometimes that works. More often, what actually drives performance is alignment. People who understand what you are trying to do, who believe in it, and who are naturally connected to the problem you are solving do not just execute better. They communicate better, sell better, and make better decisions when no one is watching. That is because they are operating from a place that is real to them.

Where this often breaks down is the ego.

Founders naturally want to believe they understand the customer, the market, the strategy, and the execution all at once. Sometimes they do. Most of the time, though, that mindset becomes the risk.

Authenticity requires you to acknowledge what you do not know. It requires you to bring in people who are closer to the problem than you are and then trust them. Not halfway. Not when it is convenient. Fully.

That can be uncomfortable, especially for entrepreneurs who are used to relying on instinct and control. But if the entire business only works when filtered through your own perspective, then what you are building is probably more fragile than you think.

In my current business, we operate in sustainability, waste, and recycling.

On the surface, this sounds like a product conversation. In reality, though, what we are really building are systems. And authenticity in that environment shows up in the most practical ways.

You can have the solar panels on your roof, and your brand claims you are committed to sustainable production, but when someone walks into your facility with a water bottle and can't figure out how to properly dispose of it sustainably, you have lost them. If that happens, all the hard work you have done behind the scenes goes to waste.

Waste is the clearest way to demonstrate your commitment to the environment in your facility. It provides a visual signal for anyone who walks through the front door. If you don't have credibility, trust is lost.

That is because authenticity lives in the experience, not in the intention.

That idea has followed me through every business I have worked in. Whether it is feeding kids, building a consumer product, or designing systems at scale, I always come back to the same question: What has to be true for this to work?

And then the more important question immediately follows: Is it actually reflected in how we operate?

Entrepreneurship has a tendency to reward what looks right. The right language, the right positioning, the right story. But over time, the businesses that last are the ones where the product, the people, the message, and the experience all tell the same story. Because the business was actually built that way from the beginning.

That is what authenticity really is. It is not a feeling, and it is not a slogan. It is a discipline. And when you get it right, it becomes one of the only things your competitors cannot copy, no matter how closely they study everything else.

CHAPTER 8

Opportunity Lives on the Edges

By Ryan Dewey Smith,
Founding Executive Chairman and CEO,
Inperium

After more than three decades of building businesses, I have come to believe that the most valuable opportunities rarely appear in the center of the field. They appear at the edges.

Most organizations spend their time focused on the obvious. They look straight ahead at what is already working, what their competitors are doing, and what the industry has always done. That is the comfortable place to operate. It is predictable and measurable. But it is also where the least innovation happens.

Entrepreneurs who want to build something meaningful have to learn to operate differently. They have to develop the ability to work in the margins, the gray areas, the places where the rules are not fully written yet.

That mindset has guided my work for more than 30 years.

I started my career in the early 1990s after graduating with degrees in psychology and business. It did not take long for me to realize that the traditional paths available to me were not where I wanted to spend my life. I wanted to build something new, something that approached human services differently.

That idea led to the founding of Supportive Concepts for Families in 1993. What started as a single organization eventually evolved into a broader vision. In 2016, I founded Inperium as a parent organization designed to bring together a diverse range of non-profit and service organizations under one strategic umbrella. Today, that platform has grown into a national organization with affiliates across more than twenty states and access to hundreds of millions of dollars in capital.

The path from a small startup to a billion-dollar enterprise was not linear.

It never is.

One of the most important lessons I learned along the way is that entrepreneurs must develop a very short memory when it comes to failure.

Think about the Wright Brothers. If they had stopped trying to build a flying machine after the first or fifth crash, aviation would not exist today. Innovation requires experimentation, and experimentation guarantees mistakes. If you cannot move past those moments quickly, you will never build anything that matters.

Framed correctly, failure is feedback. And feedback is a gift.

Most people instinctively resist negative feedback. We prefer validation. But the harsh truth is that praise rarely teaches you anything new. Criticism does. The people who question your ideas, challenge your assumptions, or point out weaknesses in your approach are often the ones giving you the information you need to improve.

So, embrace the naysayers, because they often become your most valuable source of intelligence. They force you to sharpen your thinking. They expose blind spots. They help you stress-test ideas before the market does it for you.

Entrepreneurs who treat criticism as an attack miss the opportunity hidden inside it.

The same principle applies to failure itself. If something you build is not producing the results you expected, the worst thing you can do is cling to it out of pride. One of the most important disciplines in entrepreneurship is the ability to fail fast. When an idea is not working, recognize it early, extract the lessons, and pivot.

Waiting too long can destroy momentum. Closing something down and moving to the next opportunity is often far easier than trying to revive a concept that never had the right conditions to succeed.

This ability to adapt becomes even more important as organizations grow. When Inperium began expanding across states and service lines, I quickly realized that a traditional top-down leadership model would not work.

You cannot run a decentralized organization from a single command post.

Instead, we built a constellation model of leadership. Our executive team operates as a network rather than a hierarchy. Decisions are distributed among leaders who have deep expertise in their areas, and those leaders operate with a high level of trust and autonomy. That kind of structure only works if you surround yourself with exceptional people.

One of the biggest mistakes founders make is hiring people who think exactly like they do. That creates comfort, but it limits growth. I have always tried to surround myself with people who know more than I do in specific areas and who are not afraid to challenge my thinking.

It requires humility. But it is also the only way to build an organization that can operate effectively at scale.

Even with that approach, finding the right leadership team takes time. Over the years, we have worked with many talented people, but only a fraction ultimately fit the culture and expectations required to operate in a decentralized model. Building the right team is not a one-time decision. It is an ongoing process of alignment, communication, and trust.

Another lesson I have learned is that entrepreneurs often wait too long to ask for help.

There is a cultural belief in business that independence equals strength. Founders are expected to have all the answers and solve every problem on their own. In reality, that mindset can be incredibly damaging.

Some of the strongest organizations I have seen are built through partnerships, affiliations, mergers, and collaborative structures that allow each participant to contribute their strengths.

Recognizing that you need additional expertise, resources, or systems is not a weakness. It is a strategy for sustainability. The earlier you raise your hand and ask for help, the more options you have available.

Entrepreneurship also requires a certain psychological posture toward change. If you find yourself constantly defending what you have already built, you are probably operating on defense. And organizations that remain on defense for too long become exhausted and vulnerable. Growth requires staying on offense.

It means constantly scanning the environment, expanding your field of vision, and exploring opportunities that others have not yet recognized. At Inperium, we often describe this as expanding our periphery. The more we grow, the more of the field we can see. The closer we get to a full 360-degree perspective, the more effectively we can identify emerging opportunities and risks.

That awareness only develops through experience, reflection, and an openness to learning from every outcome.

CHAPTER 9

Scaling Ideas Without Scaling Costs

By Peter Zerzan,
Filmmaker

As an independent filmmaker, I've always had a unique lens, both as the man behind the camera and as the one in the crowd. Before I ever tried to produce a movie, I worked on political campaigns. Campaigns are chaotic environments. They run on urgency, limited resources, and the constant pressure to prove progress.

What you learn very quickly in that world is that ideas alone don't win elections. Organization does. Messaging does. Discipline does.

Years later, when I began working in film, I realized the same rules applied. Yes, a film set looks vastly different from campaign headquarters, but the underlying challenge is almost identical. You're asking people to believe in something that doesn't exist yet.

In both worlds, you're building belief long before you build the final product.

Investors, producers, actors, and audiences all have to buy into a vision. They have to turn an idea into something real. In politics, the goal might be passing legislation or winning an election. In filming, the goal is to complete a project that resonates with the audience.

French director François Ozon once said something that film-makers sometimes forget: *Cinema is a business.*

It's a simple statement, but it cuts through a lot of mythology about creative industries. People imagine filmmaking as inspiration striking, a brilliant script appearing, and the rest falling into place. The reality I've seen is far less romantic. Films succeed because people organize around them. That's what has under-pinned my journey when creating my own films.

That has also defined my experiences in political campaigns, where success depends on mobilizing people with limited resources. What I've realized, more importantly, is that when an entrepreneur builds a venture of any kind, the same principles apply.

The most powerful entrepreneurs are the ones who can scale belief, structure, and alignment without scaling costs.

A lot of advice sounds like this: dream bigger, raise more money, and build a larger team. The larger assumption here is that scale creates success. But if you've spent any time around real projects, whether political campaigns or film productions, you quickly realize something uncomfortable: increasing resources without increasing discipline usually makes things worse.

I've seen campaigns with huge budgets fall apart because the structure wasn't clear. People were busy, metrics looked impressive, but nobody could explain how those activities turned into votes. The same thing happens in film. You'll occasionally meet someone who talks about a project as if the only missing ingredient is a multi-million-dollar studio check, but that's not how it works. Studios don't fund ideas. They fund teams that exhibit confidence in demonstrating those ideas. The real challenge lies in organizing the effort behind scaling an idea. That's the mindset I carried from political organizing into filmmaking.

Campaigns operate under brutal constraints. You're trying to mobilize thousands of people while tracking data, managing volunteers, and communicating a clear message, all while the clock is ticking toward Election Day. What matters most in that environment is clarity. Everyone needs to know the goal, their role, and the next action.

Filmmaking today works the same way. The old Hollywood system, a studio with lots of conveyor-belt products, largely disappeared years ago. But for a long time, there were still career pipelines. You started in one department, learned the craft, and slowly moved up.

That world has vanished.

Today, filmmakers have to act like entrepreneurs.

You have to pitch the vision, raise money, assemble teams, and convince investors that the journey itself is worth joining. That begins with honesty. As a filmmaker myself, I know firsthand the consequences of laying false promises, like claiming connections that may never materialize. All that does is erode trust and shut doors permanently.

Most investors understand that filmmaking is a risky endeavor, and pretending otherwise undermines trust. Instead, I believe in being transparent about both the risks and the opportunities. The reality is that many films do not generate significant profits. But investors still choose to participate because they believe in the project, the people behind it, and the cultural impact it might have.

In other words, they are investing in a narrative as much as a financial outcome.

And that mindset goes way beyond filmmaking. Whether you are building a technology startup, launching a manufacturing company, or producing a film, people respond to the broader vision behind what you are doing. They want to understand why the project matters and what it could become.

Another thing I've come to believe strongly is that entrepreneurs sometimes lose sight of the people they are ultimately trying to reach. It is easy to get caught up in industry jargon and big-picture language about innovation or disruption. But at the end of the day, most audiences and customers are simply trying to live their lives.

Somewhere out there is a person waking up early in the morning to go to work, worrying about paying their bills, and taking care of their family. That person is not thinking about your marketing buzzwords. They are thinking about whether what you are offering actually adds value to their life.

If your idea cannot connect with that reality, it becomes much harder to build something sustainable.

Looking back, the lessons I learned in political organizing still shape the way I approach every project. Campaigns taught me that you can summon large groups of people with limited resources if the mission is clear and the organization is disciplined. Filmmaking reinforced that lesson in a different context, proving that a strong idea supported by careful planning can accomplish far more than most people expect.

There is also one final principle that I return to often, and it comes from the late chef Anthony Bourdain. He once said that you can teach someone how to cook a steak, but you cannot teach them a work ethic.

So if I could offer any lesson to entrepreneurs building companies today, it would be this:

Treat your venture like a campaign. Start with a mission that people can rally around. Build a team that believes in it. And structure the work so that every step moves you closer to the outcome. And once you have that in place, work hard for what you believe in. Because in the end, whether you're running for office or producing a film, success usually comes down to the same thing.

Not the size of the budget, but the strength of the organization behind the idea.

CHAPTER 10

Prepare for Turbulence and Keep Flying

By Peter Miles,
President, St. Croix Wealth Management

Before founding St. Croix Wealth Management, I spent years in aviation, a world where preparation, discipline, and situational awareness are necessities. I carried that mindset from the cockpit into financial planning, where the stakes may look different, but the need for structure, judgment, and calm decision-making remains just as real. That background taught me one of the most important lessons of my entrepreneurial life: success comes from knowing how to keep moving when the plan changes.

Most people think entrepreneurship begins with the courage to take off. In reality, that is only the beginning. The harder part is what happens when circumstances you did not predict start moving against you. That is when you find out whether you are simply following a route or whether you actually know how to lead.

That is why I think entrepreneurship is best understood as a flight plan. A good pilot does not simply point the plane forward and hope for the best. There is preparation, a checklist, a destination, alternate routes, weather awareness, communication, maintenance, and an entire support structure behind every takeoff. Business is no different. Founders need a plan. They need systems. They need people they trust. They need to know where they are going and why.

But none of that means the journey will unfold exactly as expected. It never does. Turbulence is inevitable, and the entrepreneurs who succeed are the ones who are prepared for it.

That starts with a simple principle: build the plan, then prepare to revise it. One of the biggest mistakes founders make is confusing their initial vision with reality. They imagine a straight path. They assume the market will respond the way they expect, the supply chain will hold, the economy will cooperate, and every moving part will behave exactly as projected. A key process fails. A trusted assumption turns out to be wrong. In aviation, those changes are expected. In business, they should be expected, too.

The plan matters because it gives you direction. The ability to revise it matters because it keeps you alive.

That leads to the second lesson: keep flying the plane. In aviation, when something goes wrong, there is an order to how you respond. First, you aviate. Then you navigate. Then you communicate. You keep flying the airplane. You do not panic. You do not freeze. You do not become so distracted by the problem that you stop doing the fundamental thing keeping you in the air. Business works the same way. When conditions turn difficult, you still have to keep leading. You still have to keep the business moving. You still have to keep making decisions.

Aviation taught me that every landing you walk away from is a good landing. I once put a plane between two trees to take the wings off because that was the right way to reduce a greater danger. I still have the yoke from that plane on my desk, as proof of what preparation, judgment, and calm execution can do under pressure. In business, the same is true. Not every quarter will be pretty. But if you can make the hard move, protect what matters most, and keep the business intact, that matters more than appearances.

The third lesson is one many entrepreneurs resist at first: hire for your weaknesses. Founders often start because they are excellent at something specific. But being great at the core idea is not the same as being great at building and running an organization.

In a plane, the pilot is not doing everything alone. There is a co-pilot, air traffic control, mechanics, and crew, all playing critical roles. In business, it should be no different. I need to spend my time where I add the most value. That only becomes possible when the right people are in the right seats. Operations, marketing, client service, paperwork, support, scheduling, compliance, communication: every one of those functions matters. A lot of founders treat hiring like adding a liability. I think that is backwards. The right hire is an asset. The right team expands your capacity and protects your ability to grow.

The fourth lesson is just as important: ask for help before you lose control. In both aviation and entrepreneurship, overestimating your abilities can become fatal. In business, it may not look dramatic in the moment, but it can destroy a company all the same. Founders enter unfamiliar conditions all the time. New markets, new regulations, new technologies, new stages of growth. The trouble starts when they pretend to know more than they do. There is no weakness in asking for guidance. In fact, not asking is often what creates the biggest danger.

Most crashes in aviation come down to pilot error. In business, many failures do, too. Not because the founder lacked talent, but because they refused to acknowledge the limits of their own experience. They stopped listening. They stopped asking. They believed confidence alone would carry them through unfamiliar conditions. It does not work that way.

Finally, treat hard landings as lessons, not failures. Experience matters because it teaches you what no theory can. A pilot with real hours has seen things go wrong and learned how to respond. An entrepreneur who has navigated setbacks has an understanding that someone with a perfect résumé but no adversity often lacks. Mistakes, disruptions, and difficult seasons expose weaknesses, but they also reveal what needs to change.

Sometimes the storm does more than just test the business; it shows you how to build a better one.

That, to me, is the real work of entrepreneurship. Yes, it takes courage to step out and do it. It takes a little bit of craziness, too. You have to be willing to move without guarantees and keep going through the unfamiliar. But over time, the bigger challenge is having the discipline to adapt, the humility to ask for help, and the judgment to surround yourself with the right people.

A business, like a plane, stays aloft because you respect the systems, know your role, prepare for what can go wrong, and stay calm enough to lead when it does. The founders who succeed are the ones who are prepared for the turbulence and keep flying the plane when it inevitably hits.

CHAPTER 11

Building What Others Only Imagine

By Charles J. Kritter,
Founder and Inventor, KruzCup

Entrepreneurship requires two distinct modes of thinking. The first is the instinct of an inventor—the ability to recognize possibilities others overlook and imagine new solutions to everyday problems. The second is the discipline of an engineer—the structured thinking required to turn an idea into something functional and reliable.

That balance has shaped my own journey as a founder. Before starting KruzCup, much of my experience centered on product design and three-dimensional modeling. Over time, I became fascinated not just with how objects look but how they function in everyday environments. The more time you spend observing how people interact with products, the more you begin to notice small nuances.

For entrepreneurs, those everyday frictions are often where innovation begins. The concept behind KruzCup came from exactly that kind of moment.

After spending long hours driving, I began noticing something simple but surprisingly persistent. Factory cup holders rarely accommodate the wide variety of bottles, cans, and tumblers people carry with them every day. Some containers are too large, others wobble because they are too small, and many leave drivers dealing with spills or scratched interiors. It seems like a minor inconvenience on the surface, but these kinds of persistent problems often reveal opportunities for meaningful product innovation that is simply not in existence yet.

At first, the idea existed only in my head. Like many early-stage concepts, it was easy for me to visualize but difficult for others to fully understand. Anyone who has spent time around entrepreneurs knows this pattern well. A founder can clearly imagine the solution while the audience struggles to see what it might actually look like in practice.

It is in that gap between imagination and application that many ideas stall.

The turning point came when I moved the idea from concept to design. By doing so, I was able to move beyond explaining an idea and actually show people what the solution would look like. I could present something tangible.

From there, the process becomes one of refinement. Each version reveals something new about shape, materials, and usability. Some adjustments are small but important. Others require rethinking entire elements.

This stage is where the engineering mindset becomes critical. Ideas can start quickly, but turning them into something practical requires discipline, patience, iteration, and careful attention to detail. Prototypes also change how people respond to the concept. Instead of debating whether an idea might work, they begin evaluating how well it is understood to function.

For entrepreneurs who consistently find themselves stuck in the invention phase, that shift can be powerful. I get it; I've been there myself. It can be so easy to underestimate the importance of moving quickly from concept to demonstration. A working example, even a rough one, allows others to understand the value immediately.

This principle applies beyond product development. Many organizations struggle because they lean too heavily toward one side of the entrepreneurial equation. Some companies generate endless ideas but lack the operational rigor required to bring them to market. Others operate with impressive efficiency but fail to cultivate the creativity needed to develop new solutions.

Excellence in both domains leads to long-term success.

The same dynamic applies to team building. An organization driven entirely by procedures may run smoothly, but may struggle when a project's scope falls outside of any defined workflows. At the same time, a company fueled purely by enthusiasm and invention may generate energy but fail to consistently deliver results. The strongest teams manage to encourage creativity while maintaining clear systems for testing and execution. New ideas are welcomed, but they are also challenged, refined, and improved through the process.

Throughout my experience, I have connected with other innovators, founders, and entrepreneurs, and observed how they present and refine their ideas. Exposure to different environments and viewpoints gives perspective and allows you to see patterns in how products evolve from concept to market. But you also begin to appreciate how much patience the process requires.

There are three key points here to think about that can help entrepreneurs find the balance between the inventor and engineer mindsets.

First, look for friction before ideas. Strong innovation begins with paying attention to openings in an already existing process. It is the inventor's creative mindset that allows you to imagine a better possibility, but it is the engineer's practical mindset that studies why the problem exists and how it can be solved.

Second, turn concepts into something tangible. Ideas are easy to misunderstand until they take shape, so give your ideas shape. The inventor sees what could exist, while the engineer tests whether it actually works. Rough prototypes help expose weaknesses, refine the design, and communicate the idea more clearly.

And third, build teams that support both creativity and structure. Creative thinking and disciplined execution need to work together. As an entrepreneur, you should intentionally cultivate both perspectives so imagination can generate opportunities while structured processes turn them into dependable results.

Whether building a consumer product or developing a service-based company, it will be your ability to bring these two mindsets together that ultimately moves your idea from an abstract concept to something people can use creatively in their everyday lives.

And ultimately, that is the purpose of entrepreneurship: building something that improves how people interact with the world around them.

CHAPTER 12

Finance Is Not a Rear-View Mirror

By Heather Hall,
Founder and CEO,
Sapphire CFO Solutions

Entrepreneurs are driven by vision. Founders see possibilities others do not, and push forward even when the path is uncertain.

As the founder of Sapphire CFO Solutions and a finance executive with more than two decades of C-suite experience, I have worked with startups, fintech companies and mid-market organizations navigating growth, transformation, and mergers. Across those environments, I've recognized a consistent pattern. Finance is treated as an afterthought, something that simply follows the success of a product. It is treated as a reporting function rather than a strategic one, with leaders looking at the numbers to understand what already happened instead of using them to guide what should happen next.

What I've seen is that businesses rarely fail because the founder cannot build. They fail because they run out of runway.

This is where the idea of a modern CFO mindset becomes crucial for entrepreneurs.

The problem is thinking of finance as a rear-view mirror. Leaders review monthly performance to try and explain the past. While that information is important, it is only part of the story. Finance should also act as a forward-looking lens. It should help leaders understand where they are going, what risks may emerge, and what choices are available before those risks become urgent.

When companies approach finance this way, the conversation often changes. And with it, so does the perspective. Instead of asking what happened in the previous month or quarter, leaders begin asking what should be done next. That shift creates something incredibly valuable for entrepreneurs.

Optionality.

One of the greatest advantages of financial foresight is that it provides choices. Without visibility into the future, companies are forced to be reactive, and they may discover too late that hiring plans are unsustainable, that capital is running out faster than expected, or that growth initiatives are not supported by the underlying economics of the business. At that point, the only available options are often painful ones.

But it does not need to be like this. With the right financial perspective in place early, those situations look very different. You can see challenges forming before they become crises. You can evaluate trade-offs, adjust hiring plans, rethink pricing models, or delay certain investments in favor of others. Not every option will be ideal, but having multiple paths forward is always better than being forced in a single direction.

What I often tell founders is that having a set of imperfect options is better than having none at all.

This kind of clarity does more than protect a company's finances. It can reduce stress across the leadership team, because when leaders understand the financial realities of their business or department, they can plan deliberately instead of reacting under pressure. Conversations become more constructive because the team is working from the same set of data and the same shared understanding of the company's position.

That shared understanding is another key reason why the role of finance should never be isolated from the rest of the organization.

You may or may not be aware, but a modern CFO does far more than produce spreadsheets. The role requires active collaboration with leaders across the company. Finance should be integrated into discussions with operations, sales, product, and HR so that everyone is aligned around the same narrative. Unfortunately, what I often see is that financial data lives in silos, resulting in organizations working from conflicting information.

Different departments thus tell completely different stories about the same business.

Transparency solves much of that problem. The numbers stop being intimidating and become a tool that can help teams understand their next moves more clearly. And for entrepreneurs, knowing the next move can often be a huge advantage in itself.

Part of my role as a CFO is translating financial complexity into language leaders can use. Not every entrepreneur needs to know the formulas behind the model or the mechanics of the forecast. What they need is enough clarity to understand what the numbers mean, what decisions they support, and what actions should follow.

Presented this way, finance looks different. No longer a compliance exercise or monthly report, it becomes a strategic lever that gives leadership the ability to make better decisions, the confidence to move faster, and the control to scale without chaos.

This change also protects something many founders unintentionally lose sight of as they scale: their values.

I see many organizations obsess over valuation while overlooking values. This can be difficult, especially for startups and newer businesses that are finding some initial momentum. Leaders track revenue aggressively but stop paying attention to relationships, pushing for speed and growth while gradually losing sight of the purpose that originally motivated them to build the company.

I believe this often happens precisely because leaders feel trapped on a single track. When the only goal is hitting certain financial milestones or funding targets, everything else becomes secondary.

Financial clarity actually helps prevent that.

When leaders can clearly visualize their runway, their trade-offs, and their long-term options, they can make decisions with intention. They are not forced into reactive moves that compromise culture or integrity. Instead, they can build relationships and companies that grow responsibly while staying aligned with the values that define them.

Leadership is often revealed most clearly during moments of uncertainty. Titles fade and markets change, but how leaders respond to difficult decisions is what truly defines them. A strong financial foundation will never eliminate uncertainty, but it can give leaders the perspective needed to navigate with confidence.

Ultimately, finance should never exist simply to report the past. Its greatest value is helping business leaders prepare for the future. Entrepreneurs do not need to become financial experts to embrace this mindset, but they do need to recognize that financial foresight belongs at the center of strategic decision-making from the very beginning.

Numbers tell a story, but most founders have never been taught how to read it.

CHAPTER 13

Entrepreneurship Without Ownership: The Orchestrator Era

By Sarah Carson,
Actor, Private Investigator, Public Speaker,
and Former Corporate Leader

Many people still picture an entrepreneur as someone who owns the thing. The factory, the storefront, the patents, the inventory. The "assets."

But the longer I've worked across very different worlds, including corporate leadership, private investigation, and acting, the more convinced I've become that we're moving into a different era, one where the edge comes less from ownership and more from orchestration.

I'm Sarah Carson, an actor with an MBA from Harvard Business School and a background that includes senior roles in corporate banking, work as a licensed private investigator, and even time as a grain farmer. That might sound unusual on paper, but it has given me a front-row seat to a pattern that keeps repeating: the people who thrive are the ones who can assemble trust, talent, and timing faster than the world changes.

In entertainment, there's a role that explains this perfectly. Many projects don't get made because one person owns everything. They get made because a "packager" pulls together the essential elements. The packager does not own the studio, does not own the platform, and may not even "own" the idea in the way people imagine. But they can get the right people to say yes, in the right sequence, with the right expectations. That is entrepreneurial orchestration.

Once you see it, you start seeing it everywhere.

When I worked in corporate America, I watched smart people create enormous value without being the founder. One example that stuck with me was when leadership finally woke up to the fact that small-business banking was not just a nice add-on, but one of the most profitable segments. The glamorous focus had been on large corporate clients. Growth had been sitting in plain sight with the entrepreneurs. The shift required people who could reorganize priorities, retrain teams, and redesign offerings around what their market was actually doing.

I saw the same orchestration model in a much smaller setting, too. I once worked with a design-driven small business that did not own manufacturing facilities at all. The enterprise was essentially a living network of contributors and partners, assembled and reassembled as demand shifted. Traditional thinking might dismiss that as unstable. I saw the opposite: it was resilient precisely because it could bend.

And before any of that, I saw it on a farm.

I'm old enough to remember the transition from horse farming to mechanized grain farming. The new equipment was expensive. Very few individual farmers could afford to buy everything they needed on their own, so they collaborated. Several people would buy a tractor. Someone else a picker. They coordinated schedules and helped each other plant one field, and then the next, and the next.

That memory points to what I believe is becoming the signature of modern entrepreneurship: the ability to combine disparate parts without needing to own them.

But what does this really mean?

It means your "capital" is changing.

Money still matters, of course, and so do assets. But increasingly, your most renewable form of capital will be reputation: the confidence people have that you will do what you said you would do, when you said you would do it, without creating unnecessary chaos.

The idea sounds soft until you test it against real life. When I became a private investigator, I built the business through relationships and outcomes. I knew attorneys, and they knew my work. The next referral came because someone trusted that I could deliver. The thing that sustained the business was people feeling safe putting their problems in my hands.

And in the future, I believe this will become even more important. As markets fragment and teams distribute, as technology lowers barriers to entry, what will differentiate you is not simply that you exist, but that people can count on you.

Another thing to keep in mind is that orchestration requires resilience and reinvention. Many entrepreneurs still build as if the future is stable: one product, one lane, one identity, one long straight road. But the ground underneath businesses shifts faster now. New data appears, customer behavior changes fast, and tools once thought of as breakthroughs become obsolete before they are fully rolled out. Entire industries rewire.

If your business cannot pivot, it will be fragile.

In order for entrepreneurs to start orchestrating, you will need to stop romanticizing ownership and pursue mastery of the underlying architecture. One of the most practical advantages entrepreneurs have today is that they can build on top of systems that already exist, whether it's distribution channels, platforms, vendor networks, specialized contractors, shared tools, the internet, or AI.

You do not always need to build the entire machine. But you do need to understand the machine well enough to plug into it intelligently, and to pull together the pieces in a way that creates something new.

That is orchestration.

And it brings us back to the farm. Many of those farmers survived because they understood that access and coordination could viably replace ownership. They learned to share resources without losing pride. They learned to collaborate without losing independence.

That is a lesson worth carrying into this era.

Orchestrate what accelerates your impact: partnerships, talent, platforms, distribution, and the structures that let you move without carrying unnecessary weight.

Because the entrepreneurs who will be celebrated in the years ahead may not look like classic founders. They may look more like architects, conductors, or package builders. People who bring others together, protect trust, and keep adapting as the world keeps changing around them.

And if that becomes the new definition of entrepreneurship, then the good news is this: you do not need to start with a pile of assets. You can start with the right mindset, a network you treat with respect, and a reputation you guard as if it is the most valuable asset you own.

Because it might be.

CHAPTER 14

Entrepreneurship Where Others See Impossibility

By Charlene Bennett,
Co-Founder and CEO,
Individual Advocacy Group

For more than three decades, I have been building a mission-driven organization that many people still struggle to recognize as a business at all.

The organization I founded, Individual Advocacy Group (IAG), provides customized support for people with developmental, intellectual, emotional, behavioral, and neurological disabilities, helping them pursue greater independence.

Yet behind that mission sits a level of operational complexity most people never see.

Running this kind of organization means navigating intricate Medicaid billing systems, individualized allocation codes, insurance requirements, payroll, taxes, regulatory scrutiny, staffing pressure, fundraising challenges, and risk management that never truly switches off. Even a single staff member's hour of work may need to be coded differently depending on the individual being supported. Nothing is standardized. Nothing is simple.

The people we support often have complex needs that many systems avoid because the support is seen as too difficult, too intense, or too expensive. In that environment, there is no single answer that solves everything.

What you need instead is a culture of acceptance. One that rethinks housing, staffing, regulation, and belonging itself. That is the entrepreneurial lens I've developed.

If your business, service, product, or organization cowers from those with complex needs, it is convenience dressed up as courage.

Entrepreneurship is often presented through polished stories about products, scale, and opportunity. It looks clean when it is about apps, consumer brands, or high-margin services.

It looks very different when the phone rings at two in the morning because someone has jumped out of a window and is lying injured on a highway. It looks different when your revenue is largely fixed; every hour of service must be coded differently just to get paid, and the people you support are those that many providers would prefer not to take on.

That is where resilience, flexibility, and being able to solve unforeseen and complex problems either become a culture or collapse into bureaucracy and burnout.

The popular narrative of entrepreneurship says you begin with a strong idea, prove there is a market, build systems around it, and scale. That approach works well enough in industries where customers have choices, prices can change, and the stakes are mostly financial. But it breaks down quickly when you are working with people whose needs are complex and whose funding is largely determined by policy rather than pricing power.

In that world, waiting for the perfect model often becomes an excuse to avoid the hardest problems.

I have learned to see entrepreneurship differently.

In my world, there is no single program you can roll out. Every individual has different needs, different risks, and different dreams. So the daily question becomes: what would real inclusion look like for this person, and how do we design around all the reasons the system says it cannot be done?

That mindset changes how you define entrepreneurship. It becomes the willingness to reorganize resources, relationships, and regulations in the service of people others have written off.

That is what a culture of inclusion looks like in practice. It means saying yes to problems the system is built to avoid.

If you want to build that kind of culture, there are several shifts that matter.

First, redefine who counts. Too many organizations build their services around simplicity or customers that they deem predictable. In my field, the word "disability" is often used so broadly that it hides enormous differences in complexity. If you only design for the easiest cases, you are not building an inclusive system. You are building a selective one.

Second, confront constraints honestly. In my work, revenue is largely fixed by funding structures. You cannot simply raise prices to improve margins. Every service is individualized, billing is technical, and compliance demands are high. But constraints do not eliminate entrepreneurship. They sharpen it. When the rates cannot change, you have to ask what else can.

Third, build partnership muscles instead of relying on heroics. Real inclusion rarely comes from a single organization acting alone. It emerges when housing innovators, clinicians, families, regulators, and entrepreneurs work together to create solutions none of them could build independently.

Fourth, design for staff endurance. The intensity of this work is often underestimated. How do you motivate staff to keep coming back when the work is emotionally demanding and physically exhausting? An organization's mission cannot survive if the people carrying it burn out.

Fifth, accept that meaningful change will create friction. When you challenge entrenched systems or financial incentives, you will not always be welcomed for it. Entrepreneurship is often celebrated as disruption, but disruption can be uncomfortable, controversial, and deeply personal.

Entrepreneurship in this space does not look like the stories most people are used to hearing.

It requires business discipline under tight financial constraints. It requires leadership in moments of crisis. It requires operational sophistication without the luxury of easy margins.

Most of all, it requires determination.

If entrepreneurship truly means creating possibilities where none existed before, then the real test of entrepreneurship is not whether it works in the easiest situation.

It is whether it works in times of difficulty, and for the ones everyone else has already given up on.

CHAPTER 15

The Innkeeper Mindset: Build a Business People Feel

By Robert Polacek,
Co-Founder and Creative Director,
RoseBernard Studio

I have spent much of my career thinking about hospitality, but the lesson I keep coming back to has very little to do with hotels. It applies just as much to technology, finance, retail, design, healthcare, and nearly any other business that serves another human being. The lesson is this: the job is not the product, the service, or the tool. The job is the feeling the customer leaves with.

At its best, that feeling is simple. A person feels seen. Heard. Taken care of. Clear on what is happening. Free of unnecessary friction. Never abandoned in the process. Everything else—staffing, systems, design, automation, AI, process maps, scripts, platforms—is just a vehicle to deliver that outcome.

That is why I believe one of the most important shifts an entrepreneur can make is to stop asking only, "Did we follow the process?" and start asking, "Did the person feel taken care of?" That is the difference between operating a business and practicing what I think of as the "innkeeper mindset."

When I talk about the innkeeper mindset, I am not talking about nostalgia. I am not talking about returning to some romanticized version of service for its own sake. I am talking about a way of thinking that says the experience belongs to the person on the receiving end, not to the system that delivers it. If someone leaves confused, frustrated, ignored, or anxious, it does not really matter how clean the internal process was. The business may feel efficient to itself, but it has failed where it matters most.

That is where many businesses lose their way.

I do not think most companies drift from this because they stop caring. I think they drift because they grow. Founders begin close to the customer. But as the company scales, systems replace judgment. Metrics replace care. The language changes. Customers become users, tickets, cases, or categories. The minute a person becomes a category, the innkeeper's mindset is lost.

That is the entrepreneurial challenge hidden inside growth. Scale creates distance. Distance creates abstraction. And abstraction makes it easy to forget what people actually need from you.

What they need, more often than not, is not perfection. It is reassurance.

That is why I believe entrepreneurs should own the outcome, not just the process. Processes matter. Tools matter. Automation matters. But those things are only useful if they reduce friction and increase clarity. They cannot become the point. A beautifully designed system that leaves someone feeling alone is still a bad system. An automated message that is technically accurate but emotionally empty still creates distance.

This is not an argument against technology. It is an argument against hiding behind it.

If AI helps a customer gain clarity faster, lowers anxiety, and creates a smoother path, then it is serving the right purpose. If it simply allows the company to process more people while making each one feel less understood, then it is doing the opposite. The same is true of scripts, workflows, and internal systems. They should make care easier to deliver, not easier to avoid.

For entrepreneurs, this has to become a core principle: design every touchpoint so the customer never feels alone.

That can mean different things in different businesses. In a digital platform, it may mean removing confusion and making the next step obvious. In a financial service, it may mean making clients feel informed and supported rather than intimidated. In a physical environment, it may mean creating spaces that feel intuitive, calm, and human. In every case, the work is the same. Help the person feel that someone is paying attention.

That last part matters more than many leaders realize. A customer can forgive a mistake more easily than they can forgive indifference.

A new brand can recover.

A cold one cannot.

One of the advantages of operating with this mindset is that it humanizes a company. It gives a business the ability to be real, to acknowledge mistakes, and to correct course, all while keeping trust intact.

But this mindset has to start inside the business.

You cannot build a frictionless customer experience with a friction-filled team. If employees feel unsupported, unclear, or overwhelmed, they will pass that instability along. Maybe not intentionally, but inevitably. Leadership sets the tone of care. Teams mirror the system they operate in. If you want people outside the company to feel taken care of, the people inside the company need to know what that feels like first.

That is why the innkeeper mindset is also a leadership model. It asks leaders to create environments where employees are clear on what matters, where support exists before burnout takes over, and where care is not treated as softness but as operational strength. When the internal experience is grounded, the external experience gets stronger. When employees experience less friction, customers usually do too.

There is also a hard business case for this.

Without this mindset, companies tend to compete on price because they have little else left to differentiate themselves. Loyalty weakens. Churn rises. Growth becomes dependent on constant acquisition. But when people feel genuinely supported, they come back. Trust compounds. Word of mouth increases. The brand can sustain premium positioning because the experience carries emotional value, not just transactional utility.

That is the part many entrepreneurs forget when the noise gets louder. Suddenly, the business is reacting rather than remembering. By contrast, the companies that last usually know exactly who they are. Sometimes that comes down to staying true to a core message. Sometimes it is as simple as remaining simple. When businesses lose that center, they drown with everyone else. When they keep it, they stand apart.

For me, the innkeeper mindset is ultimately about that center.

It is about remembering that every system serves a person.

Every product lands in a human life.

Every interaction leaves a residue, whether it is designed or not.

Entrepreneurs who understand this do not just deliver outcomes. They deliver clarity, trust, and a sense of being cared for.

And that is what people remember.

CHAPTER 16

Narrative Is Infrastructure

By Justin Colombik,
Co-Founder and Design Director,
RoseBernard Studio

I have spent close to 20 years designing hospitality interiors across a wide range of restaurants and hotels, always working at the nexus of creativity and function. This has shaped the way I think about space. Buildings need to feel coherent, operate well, and connect with people in a way that feels natural and lasting. It has also taught me an important business lesson: the strongest creative work begins with a narrative strong enough to hold every decision together.

Story is what gives the work coherence. It tells you why something belongs, what should happen next, and how all the parts should come together. Without that, you may still end up with something attractive, but it will often feel generic.

Over time, I came to understand that the strongest work always had a narrative underneath it, which led to surprising outcomes. It made the process more disciplined. It helped the team align. It helped the client understand what they were buying. It helped the final project feel specific to its place instead of looking like it had been dropped in from somewhere else.

Start with the story, not the style. This lesson matters beyond design.

Too many businesses begin at the surface level. They ask what looks good, what is trending, or what feels safe to repeat. That may be enough to get something into the market, but it is not enough to make it meaningful.

When we begin a project, we start by looking at context. Where is the building? What is around it? What history does it carry? What kind of guest experience should be created? We build image boards, visual references, and a narrative that acts as a North Star. Once that story is clear, the design process becomes stronger because every choice has a reason behind it.

This is why I advise others to use narrative as their decision-making framework.

A good story tells you when something belongs and when it does not. It gives the team a shared language. It allows you to look at a concept board, a floorplan, a rendering, or a detail and ask a simple question: Does this still feel true to what we said we were creating? If the answer is no, then you are off course. Entrepreneurs talk constantly about vision, but vision without a framework is just instinct. A narrative makes the vision usable.

It also makes the business more persuasive. If you can explain, visually and verbally, why something should feel a certain way, why a color matters, why a material belongs, why a sequence of spaces has been arranged this way instead of that, they stop reacting only to taste and start buying into the larger idea.

That applies just as much to entrepreneurship as it does to design. Plenty of people are qualified. Plenty of people can technically do the work. But clients, customers, and partners are rarely buying a qualification alone. They are buying your point of view, how you think, how you communicate, and whether they trust your process. Storytelling is part of how we pitch, lead, and differentiate ourselves from firms that may look similar from the outside.

Seeing the impact this can have has taught me something else: to carry the story through every touchpoint.

If the narrative is strong, it should not stop at the wallpaper. It should shape the shelf display, the menu logic, the brand language, the guest experience, and the emotional tone of the space. In a restaurant, whether it's the menu design, the table layout, or the lighting, it should reinforce the larger identity. While in a hotel, that very first moment you walk through the door needs to give you a sense of place. From the check-in experience to the welcoming atmosphere, you need to feel a sense of connection to the larger narrative.

When that narrative is missing, the damage is real. The project may look polished, but it starts to feel interchangeable. It becomes a style repeated for the sake of style. It becomes something trendy rather than something rooted. In design, that often means a space that looks like everywhere else and belongs nowhere. More broadly, in business, it means a company that can operate but cannot really stand out.

That is why I believe entrepreneurs should build for specificity, not generic appeal.

Specificity is what makes a project feel authentic to a location, a customer, or a cultural context. It is what makes people remember it. It is what gives a business texture and identity. And paradoxically, the more specific you are, the more broadly people often connect to the work, because it feels real rather than manufactured.

At the heart of all this is one final lesson: differentiate through process, not just polish.

It is easy to say you have better taste. It is much harder to build a better method. What makes our studio different is that we have been more integrated, more narrative-driven, and more intentional from the beginning. That process leads to stronger work, clearer communication, and a more unified result. Entrepreneurs in any field can take something from that. There is an advantage in having a shinier product, but it is limited. The true advantage is having a deeper framework that makes every part of the business sharper.

That is what I have learned over time. The story is not there to decorate the work. It is there to hold it together. It gives the project meaning, the team alignment, the client confidence, and the final experience a sense of place and purpose. In crowded markets, that kind of clarity matters. It is what helps a business rise above repetition and create something people remember.

And the entrepreneurs who understand that will always build something stronger than those who follow style alone.

CHAPTER 17

Where Systems Stop, Entrepreneurs Start

By Rachael Rivero,
Founder, Kansas Care Connect

One of the most important lessons I have learned as an entrepreneur is that the biggest opportunities usually appear in places where established systems are rarely designed to look. They appear in the gaps.

I discovered one of those gaps in healthcare. As a nurse practitioner and founder of Kansas Care Connect, I kept seeing the same pattern: healthcare revolves around appointments, yet most health management happens between appointments. Kansas Care Connect grew out of that realization, but the lesson extends beyond healthcare.

For entrepreneurs, the real opportunity lies less in what systems already do well and more in identifying what they ignore.

For me, the clue that something was missing came from a pattern I could not ignore. Medication changes, confusion about diagnoses, missed follow-ups, juggling multiple providers, and the daily realities of chronic illness unfolded between appointments, often without guidance. Providers usually felt they had explained everything clearly, while patients often felt unsure about what to do next.

Individually, these situations look like isolated problems. Repeated across hundreds of patients, they revealed something larger: opportunity. Over time, I realized there was a simple process to follow to help gauge the scope of the opportunity.

First, as I said, notice the pattern. When the same frustration or inefficiency appears repeatedly, it isn't random. Then, ask why it exists. Sometimes, a solution already exists but is poorly implemented; other times, the system itself is structured in a way that allows the problem to continue. Finally, build around the gap. If the pattern keeps appearing and no one has addressed it effectively, that gap is probably an opportunity to explore.

Kansas Care Connect grew out of that process. Once I began asking why these issues kept appearing, the answer became clear. The healthcare system is highly organized around appointments, but it assumes that once patients leave the clinic, the plan will unfold as expected.

In reality, that is when many challenges actually begin.

Patients may not fully understand their diagnosis. They may struggle to follow new medication plans. Instructions can be forgotten, misunderstood, or difficult to implement in everyday life. For people managing chronic illness, those small breakdowns quickly compound into larger problems.

At some point, I realized something else that changed the way I looked at entrepreneurship entirely. The system itself was not broken due to people not caring. Doctors cared deeply, as did patients and administrators. The issue was that the system had never been designed to manage what happens between visits. Once I saw that clearly, the opportunity became obvious.

Building a business around that insight reinforced several lessons that I believe apply across industries.

First, test your assumptions against reality. Systems often appear logical on paper, but the real experience of the people using them can be very different. The most valuable insights often come from paying attention to how things actually work in practice.

Second, identify where systems stop paying attention. Every industry has areas that receive less focus simply because they fall outside the core process. Those overlooked spaces are often where meaningful innovation happens.

Third, expect resistance. Even when people recognize a problem, they may hesitate when someone proposes a new way of addressing it. Entrepreneurs have to be prepared to explain how their solution fits into the existing system and why it helps strengthen it.

Part of that resistance simply comes from the way people naturally respond to change. When a system has operated a certain way for years, even small adjustments can feel disruptive. In many industries, including healthcare, people learn to work within the constraints they are given, and over time, those constraints begin to feel permanent. They are not.

For entrepreneurs, this creates an unusual dynamic. You may be pointing out a problem that many people already recognize, and yet no one seems interested in the solution. Often, this is not because the idea is flawed, but because the idea challenges routines, incentives, or assumptions people have grown accustomed to.

This is why building something new requires more than simply identifying the gap. It requires patience and communication. Entrepreneurs have to help others see the world as it could be, to show that what they are building may not replace the existing structure but strengthen it where it is weakest.

When people begin to see that clearly, the resistance often fades. Looking back, Kansas Care Connect did not begin with a grand plan to transform healthcare. It began with noticing a pattern and asking a simple question: What can I do to change that?

Part of your role as an entrepreneur is learning to see what systems overlook. Because often, the next opportunity is sitting exactly there, waiting for someone to take notice.

CHAPTER 18

The Difference Between a Network and a Partner

By Danica Bilicich-Mason,
Founder and Principal, Red Team Go

One of the most common phrases in business today is "we're a relationship-based company."

You hear it everywhere. Entrepreneurs say it in interviews. Companies say it in proposals. Leaders write it on their websites and repeat it on conference stages. At this point, it has become such a familiar phrase that it almost risks losing its meaning.

Relationships absolutely matter in business. In many cases, they matter more than anything else. But most people misunderstand what a real relationship actually looks like.

Over the last sixteen years building Red Team Go, relationships have been the single biggest driver of our success. We have never relied on traditional advertising. Nearly all of our work has come through referrals and word of mouth. People often hear that and assume it means we have a large network.

In reality, it means something very different.

A network is simply a collection of contacts. A relationship is something deeper. It is built through shared values, mutual respect, and consistent follow-through over time. One can be created in minutes. The other takes years to earn.

Understanding that difference is one of the most important lessons I've learned as an entrepreneur.

Red Team Go works primarily with clients in the architecture, engineering, and construction industry, helping them craft winning proposals, develop inclusion strategies, and navigate complex civil rights programs on major infrastructure projects. The work itself is technical and often high stakes, but the foundation of our business has always been trust.

And trust doesn't come from a LinkedIn connection request. It comes from showing up prepared, doing excellent work, and respecting the people you collaborate with.

In my experience, the strongest relationships in business start by identifying people who share similar goals and values. That alignment matters far more than titles or company size.

As a small business owner, especially in an industry like construction where women are still significantly underrepresented, I learned very early that the people who would help shape my career weren't necessarily who others expected them to be. In fact, many of the most important advocates and allies I've had throughout my career have been men in the construction industry who believed in what we were building and were willing to open doors.

Those opportunities came from consistently doing good work, demonstrating reliability, and building genuine professional respect over time. That's when something interesting begins to happen. The relationship starts to extend beyond a single project.

Someone you worked with years ago moves to a new company and calls you again. A colleague recommends you to a team that needs help. A partner introduces you to someone else in their network because they trust the work you do.

At that point, the relationship stops being transactional and starts becoming something far more valuable: a long-term professional alliance. But recognizing those partnerships requires paying attention to the small signals that reveal whether a relationship is real or performative.

In the early stages of a project, many people appear aligned. Everyone is enthusiastic. Everyone says the right things. But as the work progresses, you start to notice patterns.

For example, if you send important materials before a meeting and someone consistently shows up having never reviewed them, that's not just a scheduling issue. It's a sign that they don't respect the time and effort you invested in preparing that work.

Entrepreneurs often excuse behavior like that by saying, "I'm busy." But *everyone* in business is busy. Real partnerships are built on mutual respect. If someone repeatedly fails to show that respect, it eventually becomes clear that the relationship isn't what it appeared to be.

And that realization matters, because not all relationships should continue indefinitely.

The entrepreneurs who build lasting companies are the ones who learn how to identify and nurture the right partnerships while letting go of the wrong ones. That ability becomes even more important when working with other small businesses.

Throughout my career, Red Team Go has collaborated with many smaller firms that were still building their capacity. In some cases, that meant adjusting how we structured our work or even absorbing some costs on early projects to help establish the partnership.

From a purely short-term financial perspective, that approach doesn't always look efficient.

From a long-term relationship perspective, it can be incredibly powerful.

Many of those smaller companies eventually grow. And when they do, they remember who supported them when they were still finding their footing. They introduce you to new clients.

They bring you into new projects. They become some of your strongest advocates. Over time, those partnerships create an ecosystem of trust that no marketing strategy can replicate.

But this lesson works in both directions.

Entrepreneurs often spend a lot of time evaluating whether other people are good partners. What they forget to ask is an equally important question: Are you the kind of partner others want to work with?

Do you respect the time of the people you collaborate with? Do you deliver on your commitments? Do you prioritize quality over volume?

If the answer to those questions is no, then no amount of networking will produce meaningful relationships. You cannot expect others to advocate for you, recommend you, or bring you new opportunities if you are not consistently demonstrating the same level of professionalism and respect.

The strongest professional relationships are built through reciprocity. Both sides contribute. Both sides benefit. And both sides invest in making the partnership work.

In a world increasingly obsessed with scale, follower counts, and the size of someone's network, it's easy to forget that business success rarely comes from the number of people you know.

It comes from the handful of people who truly trust you. Those are the partners who introduce you to the next opportunity. Those are the advocates who bring your name into rooms you've never entered. And those are the relationships that sustain a business long after the first project is complete.

CHAPTER 19

Before You Can Deliver Value, Define It

By Virgil Hughes,
Founder and President,
NewVines International

Entrepreneurs are often taught to move fast. Test and launch quickly, iterate even faster. But after decades working in both corporate turnarounds and social impact organizations, I have come to realize an important lesson about managing impact: before you can deliver value, you must first define it.

It may sound obvious, but for some reason, many entrepreneurs skip this step entirely. They chase funding and scale without stopping to ask the simple question: what does value actually mean to the people we serve? If it is not answered clearly, businesses can end up optimizing for the wrong outcomes.

Earlier in my career, I spent years doing turnaround work in senior care organizations. In that environment, defining value meant understanding what mattered most to residents and their families. The answers were not complicated. People wanted clean rooms and for maintenance to respond quickly. They wanted hot food hot, and cold food cold. Families wanted to know their loved ones were treated with dignity and care.

Those are tangible definitions of value.

But what I often saw was management focusing on internal metrics that had little connection to the customer experience. One example in healthcare is tracking inventory turns. They matter for cashflow, but no customer wakes up and says, "I hope this company has excellent inventory turnover." When leadership teams obsess over internal metrics that customers never feel, they risk steering away from the real source of value.

In my experience, entrepreneurs fall into this trap all the time. Founders become focused on fundraising milestones, valuation, or operational efficiency, while losing sight of the one thing that actually determines survival: whether or not the customers genuinely experience value in the product or service.

When I transitioned into social impact work through NewVines International, I realized that defining value was even more complex. There are at least two audiences: the people whose lives you are trying to improve, and the donors funding that work. For the person receiving support, value might mean food security or clean water. But for a donor, value is different. They want evidence that their contribution is meaningfully changing lives.

At first glance, those two perspectives seem like distinct definitions of value. But the challenge for any organization, nonprofit or otherwise, is finding the intersection between different types of value.

I realized early on that there was simply no way I could give away enough money to lift people out of poverty. It just does not work that way. Instead, what we can do is to provide tools, training, and systems that allow people to build a different future for themselves.

That realization led me somewhere many entrepreneurs avoid: deep into the daily realities of the people they are trying to serve.

When I started working in East Africa, I chose to live alongside the communities we were supporting. I stayed in mud huts, bathed in rivers, ate food cooked over open fires, and breathed the smoke that filled the homes. For the first five years, I refused to stay in any but the lowest-priced hotels because the people around me stayed there. I wanted to understand their world on their terms.

I remember seeing a thirteen-year-old girl in the hill country of Kenya, who had to walk a mile down the hill to get water, carrying it back up in a 20-gallon carboy for the orphanage where she lived.

When you witness something like that, it changes how you design solutions.

This is also where entrepreneurs can make a costly mistake. They assume the solution that worked in one context will work everywhere. Take microlending as an example. The model sparked a movement, and organizations rushed to replicate it across the developing world. Many focused on the banker's definition of value: loans issued, repayment rates, and efficiency. However, in my villages across East Africa, the phrase "microlender" triggers hostility. Because when loans were introduced without understanding cultural dynamics around debt and collateral, families lost homes, and what little they owned was repossessed.

Entrepreneurs make a similar mistake all the time. They see a model that worked and assume it will translate. They build products based on assumptions rather than immersion.

So, how can you avoid this? At NewVines, we were forced to approach the problem differently. Over time, we identified a set of behaviors that usually signal a real shift in mindset. When individuals began practicing several of these behaviors consistently, their lives began to change in measurable ways. This becomes valuable to them. For the donors, there is value too, because we can demonstrate real transformation, not just activity.

Let's use a common analogy, the iceberg: a small piece above the water, a huge chunk below. The programs we offer are the small, visible piece above the water: training, coaching, and practical tools. But the deeper work happens, well, deeper, below the water. That is where culture, ethics, and mindset shape the decisions people make every day.

If entrepreneurs want to build organizations that last, that deliver real value, they must pay attention to that deeper layer as well.

This also shapes how organizations should operate. Allow the people on the ground to define the value. Because when front-line leaders understand their own results, they can adapt faster and teach more effectively. Similarly, for entrepreneurs, if you become disconnected from your customers, your real value disappears.

So, if I could offer one lesson to entrepreneurs building companies today, it would be this.

Put the time in.

Spend enough time with your customers to understand what actually improves their lives or businesses. Define value clearly and in practical terms before you build systems to capitalize on it. Because when value is poorly defined, you will waste time, burn capital, and sometimes even alienate the people you hope to serve.

CHAPTER 20

Entrepreneurs Should Think Like Toy Inventors

By Dan Klitsner,
Toy Inventor and Creator of *Bop It!*

Entrepreneurship is usually framed around a familiar piece of advice: find a problem and solve it. Many of the world's most successful companies were built exactly that way. Identify a pain point, remove friction, and create something faster, easier, or more efficient. It is sound advice.

But the toy industry operates according to a completely different philosophy.

Rather than solving problems, toy inventors create them.

At first, that sounds counterintuitive. Yet nearly every toy, game, or puzzle is built on exactly this principle. Instead of eliminating difficulty, it introduces a challenge. Instead of smoothing the path forward, it invites the user to figure something out. The goal is engagement.

When you move from asking "How do I solve a problem?" to asking "How do I create an interesting challenge?", you begin to see opportunity in entirely new places.

When describing toy invention, I often use the phrase: watch the player, not the toy.

Most entrepreneurs focus their attention on the product itself. They refine features, optimize performance, and polish the mechanics of how something works. Toy inventors approach the problem from another angle. We start by watching people.

What action can we create? What behavior can we animate?

If the person interacting with the product becomes engaged, curious, or physically involved, then the design is working. The product becomes a catalyst for an experience rather than just an object.

This mindset led directly to one of my best-known inventions: *Bop It!*

The idea that turned into *Bop It!* began with a question: What if a TV remote control were actually fun to watch someone use?

Instead of a passive device where a user presses buttons to change channels, I imagined something playful and physical, called the "Channel Bopper", that the user had to twist, pull, or bop to change channels. Something that brought the person using it to life through movement and reaction.

That simple shift in thinking ultimately turned into *Bop It!*, a game that has sold tens of millions of units worldwide.

There is a deeper level to this as well.

One of the most overlooked truths about products and services is that the experience rarely belongs only to the user. It also belongs to the observer. Think about a group of people watching someone play a game. If the player is laughing, moving, reacting, and struggling to keep up, everyone around them becomes engaged too. They lean in. They want to try it.

Entrepreneurs often think primarily about the end user. But in many cases, the people watching the experience are just as important. When the person using the product is interesting to observe, it spreads naturally. Curiosity turns into participation.

This principle shaped another co-creation of mine, *Perplexus*, a spherical maze game. Instead of a traditional flat puzzle, the maze exists inside a clear sphere that players must rotate and maneuver in every direction.

Watching someone attempt to navigate the maze becomes part of the entertainment. The tension of balancing the ball, the sudden drop when it falls off track, and the physical movement required to guide it forward. The player becomes the show.

When a product animates people in this way, it naturally attracts attention. Others want to experience the challenge themselves.

That is how virality forms.

Most entrepreneurs build businesses by reducing pain points. Ride-sharing platforms remove the frustration of hailing a cab. Payment apps simplify transactions. Software automates tasks that once required hours of manual work. These are powerful innovations, and many industries depend on them.

But there is another lens entrepreneurs can apply, even in businesses far removed from toys. It requires entrepreneurs to ask a different question: What if this product were a toy? Not literally, but conceptually. What if its purpose were to engage people rather than simply serve them? What if the experience itself were memorable?

This mindset can apply to almost any business environment. It's the same thinking that turns a retail experience into an invitation to participate instead of just passive browsing. Or how presentations that challenge the audience engage them better than those that simply deliver information. And how a product demonstration is always more successful when it is interactive instead of a technical explanation.

When people feel engaged, they remember the experience. They talk about it. They share it with others. For new toys and for businesses just starting out, that is often where real growth begins.

But the biggest problem for most entrepreneurs is not coming up with ideas; it is deciding which ones they should invest their time and enthusiasm in.

Over the years, I developed a simple framework to evaluate opportunities. I call it the RITE test, and it focuses on four factors: Relationship, Idea, Timing, and Execution.

Relationship refers to the partnerships or networks required to bring the idea to life.

Idea measures whether the concept itself is truly compelling or differentiated.

Timing considers whether the market is ready for it.

Execution asks whether the team has the ability to actually build and deliver it.

Think of these four elements as the legs of a table. If one leg is weak, the entire structure becomes unstable. An entrepreneur may fall in love with an idea, but if timing or execution is lacking, the concept may struggle no matter how creative it is.

Evaluating ideas through this lens helps me identify which opportunities are truly worth pursuing. It may be useful for you, too.

After more than three decades of inventing toys and games, the question that still drives me is simple: What magic moment will this create? Whenever I imagine a new product, I picture the people using it. Kids laughing together. Families gathered around a table. Friends competing during game night.

Those moments are powerful because they bring people together.

They also demonstrate something important about entrepreneurship. Products designed to create meaningful experiences often become enduring businesses. Over the years, the toys and games I've helped invent have generated billions of dollars in sales and reached millions of households around the world.

But the real measure of success is the memories those products helped create.

That is the essence of thinking like a toy inventor. Instead of asking only how to remove problems from the world, ask how you might create moments of curiosity, interaction, and joy.

Because sometimes the most powerful entrepreneurial skill is not solving a problem, but creating one that people are excited to play with.

CHAPTER 21

Co-Creation: The Secret to Lasting Loyalty

By Kimmylea Konsel-Taylor,
Founder, LimeLight Expressions

One of the biggest misconceptions in entrepreneurship is that success comes from having the best idea. In reality, success usually comes from understanding people better than anyone else. That lesson became clear to me through LimeLight Expressions. I learned it by standing in rooms with clients, listening carefully to what they thought they wanted, and slowly discovering what they actually needed.

The difference between those two things is what separates the good from the truly memorable.

When someone hires LimeLight Expressions to design an event, they usually arrive with a basic idea. Sometimes it is very specific, but many times it is just a feeling they are trying to create. Our job is not simply to execute what they ask for, but to listen carefully enough to understand the experience they are really hoping to create.

For entrepreneurs, that listening process is where the real work begins. For us, in events, we start by asking questions. What matters most to you about this event? What kind of energy do you want your guests to feel? What details matter to you personally? Once we understand that, my team goes out and does the research. We negotiate with vendors, explore design concepts, and build out ideas that bring their vision to life. Then we bring everything back and walk through it together.

Some clients want to be involved in every step. Others prefer to step back and trust us. Either way, they remain part of the process. That collaborative approach, what I think of as co-creation, is one of the most powerful business lessons I have learned.

When clients feel involved, they feel ownership. When they feel ownership, they trust you. And trust is what turns a single project into a long-term relationship.

I saw this clearly in a particularly memorable event we designed for a family celebrating two milestone birthdays, a 50th and an 80th. The event happened to fall on Valentine's Day, and the family wanted to incorporate Chinese cultural elements because many of the guests were Chinese diplomats. The immediate challenge became color.

The daughter loved soft blush tones, while her mother-in-law preferred traditional red. Because they were not sure how those two visions could exist in the same space, we started building a concept that honored both.

Even then, the client told me she was not entirely sure how it would all come together. That moment happens often in entrepreneurship. A client gives you direction, but they cannot yet see the outcome. They are trusting you to bridge that gap.

And when you do, the reactions are incredibly rewarding—but they are also a reminder of something deeper about business. Customers rarely know the full solution they are looking for. What they do know, though, is how they want to *feel*. The entrepreneur's role is to translate that feeling into something real.

That principle extends far beyond events. Whether you are building a product, offering a service, or launching a brand, people are often reacting to an outcome they want, not necessarily the exact mechanics that will get them there. They might come to you asking for one specific thing, but what they are really after is confidence, ease, relief, joy, excitement, or connection.

If you only listen to the literal request, you may miss the bigger opportunity. If you listen closely enough to understand the emotion behind it, however, you can build something far more meaningful.

Part of being an entrepreneur is knowing when to guide the conversation. Clients will sometimes ask for something that does not quite work in the space or timeline they are imagining. When that happens, I step into the role they hired me for: the expert.

I explain the reasoning behind a different approach. Maybe the room layout will flow better another way. Maybe a moment in the timeline needs to shift to create a stronger emotional impact. This process is not about rejecting their ideas, but about helping them achieve the outcome they actually want.

That balance, listening deeply while still providing leadership, is one of the hardest skills entrepreneurs develop. Too many businesses fall into one of two traps: they either ignore the customer's voice entirely or they surrender their expertise completely. Neither works. The strongest businesses do both. They listen carefully, then elevate the idea. They create something alongside the client, but they also bring enough confidence and perspective to lead the process well.

Over time, I realized this approach was doing something powerful for our company. Clients were not just hiring us for a single event; they were coming back.

Someone who hired us for a birthday celebration might call us again for a wedding, a corporate gathering, or another family milestone. Many of our new clients arrive because someone else told them about an experience we helped create. That is why I believe word of mouth still drives some of the strongest businesses in the world. It does not come from transactions. It comes from relationships.

If there are two practical habits that have helped me most in building LimeLight Expressions, they would be these.

First, listen more than you speak. Entrepreneurs often feel pressure to present answers quickly, but the more time you spend understanding what people truly care about, the better your solution will be. Sometimes, the most valuable thing you can do for a client is simply to hear them clearly.

Second, focus on the experience, not just the outcome. A beautiful event matters, but the process leading up to that event matters just as much. When clients feel supported, informed, and respected throughout the journey, they remember the entire experience, not just the final reveal.

At the heart of my work is a simple belief: life moves fast, and the moments we celebrate together matter. When someone asks us to design an event, they are trusting us with a memory. They are trusting us to create something meaningful for the people they care about. That responsibility keeps me grounded as an entrepreneur, because in the end, the most successful businesses are the ones that build something meaningful alongside the people they serve.

CHAPTER 22

The 90 Percent They Never See

By Beau Taylor,
Security and Crew Director,
LimeLight Expressions

As a police officer and longtime SWAT team member, I have spent years working in environments where preparation and calm under pressure are not optional. I have also spent years supporting my wife's event business behind the scenes, helping turn her ideas into experiences that feel seamless to the people attending them. Those two worlds may seem different, but they have taught me the same lesson: success usually depends on the work no one else sees.

One of the biggest things I have learned in business is that the client only ever experiences a small percentage of what makes something successful. They see the final result and assume it all came together as planned. What they do not see is the contingency planning, the logistics, the vendor coordination, the problem-solving, and the adjustments happening in real time to protect that experience.

My wife is the creative force. She sees the big picture, the emotional tone, and the final experience before anyone else can. My role is to help make sure that vision can happen. Sometimes that means solving technical problems. Sometimes it means coordinating logistics. Sometimes it means anticipating issues before anyone else notices them. But it always means supporting the vision rather than detracting from it.

That has taught me something I think entrepreneurs in any industry can use: a great business is not defined only by what it produces. It is defined by how well it protects the experience from everything that could go wrong.

My wife usually says there are two things you cannot control: weather and people. That line has stayed with me because it applies to almost every business. You can have a great plan, but the minute real conditions and real people get involved, certainty disappears. Vendors run late, venues fall short, the weather shifts, and timelines compress. Someone misses a step, and suddenly the next three moving pieces are affected.

The lesson in that is simple: never build a plan that assumes ideal conditions.

If an event is outside, you do not just plan the outdoor version. You plan the backup location, the transition process, and the way to move everyone there without ruining the experience. If a major installation needs power, you do not just assume the venue can handle it. You think through electrical load, generators, routing, and backup supply. If a setup depends on multiple vendors arriving in sequence, you do not just trust that everything will go smoothly. You prepare for what happens if it does not.

That instinct comes naturally to me because I grew up in the trades. From a young age, I was around worksites where the expectation was always to figure out a way to get the job done. Later, law enforcement sharpened that mindset even more. On the SWAT team, I learned that no matter how detailed the plan is, it is never going to unfold exactly the way you pictured it.

What matters is your ability to adjust.

In my world, we call that tactical flexibility. Entrepreneurs need more of it. A lot of people think planning means predicting the future correctly. It does not. Planning means preparing yourself to adapt without losing control. So another lesson I would pass on is: build your backup plans before you need them.

For me, that often means thinking in layers. There is the original plan, then the secondary plan, then the tertiary plan. If something goes sideways, I do not want to start inventing solutions under pressure if I can avoid it. I want options ready. The more prepared you are, the smoother the pivot feels. And if you do your job well, the client never even realizes there was a pivot.

That may be the clearest sign of strong execution: people experience calm while you are solving chaos.

I have also learned a lot from the way my wife leads. She starts with the vision. She sees what the end product needs to feel like. Then I help break that vision down into the practical steps required to get there. That process has taught me another lesson entrepreneurs can use: turn the big idea into executable steps.

A lot of people can describe what they want. Far fewer can identify the exact sequence required to make it real. Even fewer can do that while staying flexible enough to adjust when one of those steps fails. That is why execution matters as much as vision. A business does not succeed because the idea sounds good. It succeeds because somebody is making sure every moving piece is working toward the same outcome.

Another part of that is managing people well. Vendors, contractors, team members, and venue staff are all part of the equation, and every one of them can affect the outcome. So, set expectations early, but stay ready to adjust.

Clients usually never see this, because our job is to stop the disruption before it reaches them. That is part of what leadership behind the scenes looks like. You are not just managing tasks. You are managing momentum.

And finally, the most important thing I have learned is this: put out the fire before anyone smells the smoke.

Clients do not need to know every problem that arises. They do not need to know whether you ended up on Plan A, Plan B, or

Plan C. They just need to feel that they were taken care of. If we have done our job right, they walk away saying everything was perfect. They never know how much had to be adjusted to make it feel that way.

That, to me, is what great entrepreneurship looks like behind the scenes. People celebrate the visible 10 percent, the event, the product, the result. But the real difference is made in the other 90 percent: the discipline, the flexibility, the contingency planning, the calm under pressure, and the commitment to making someone's dream come true without them ever realizing how it happened.

That is the part clients may never see.

But it is the part they always feel.

CHAPTER 23

Beyond Breakthrough: Invention as Enduring Culture

By George Abetti,
Founder, Geobarns

Before Geobarns, I was an ordained minister. When I founded Geobarns in the early 1990s, I saw it as a continuation of service and stewardship. Building homes became another way of serving people at one of the most significant moments of their lives.

Over the past three decades, our company has grown from a single creative breakthrough into a respected design-build operation. To some, what defines Geobarns today is our architectural style and the structural integrity of our builds. But what has always mattered most to me is that innovation did not remain a singular event in our history. It became part of our culture, something lived, protected, and passed on through our people.

If you've ever started a business, you might remember the breakthrough. The first idea that worked, the first client who believed in you. But what happens after that first success can often determine whether you were inventive or just lucky.

For entrepreneurs, it becomes crucial to understand how invention can move from a single breakthrough to an enduring culture, and why many founder-led businesses lose their edge once the original inventor steps back.

Many of us believe that moments of creative brilliance belong to the inventor, to individuals. We picture a lone creator with a breakthrough idea, and we assume that the idea, or belief in the idea, is what sustains a company. The advice that follows is predictable: protect the idea, scale it, and replicate it. Then defend it.

It sounds right, but it creates a fragile business.

When the idea is tied to one person or one defining moment, the company can become overly dependent on that individual. Once the founder steps back, retires, or loses their drive, the spark fades. What often remains is a competent organization, but no longer a dynamic one.

As the adage goes, "Pioneers usually make terrible settlers."

The real question entrepreneurs should be asking is whether the company itself has learned how to invent. What leads to sustained success is not the breakthrough moment but the discipline behind the idea. It's the willingness to sacrifice preference for improvement, and the humility to adjust what has always worked in order to serve someone better. It is the habit of asking, again and again, how something could be done more thoughtfully.

Viewed this way, invention becomes the company's operating principle. It moves from personality to practice. From charisma to culture.

The company no longer relies on one creative mind but builds shared standards, shared sacrifice, and shared ownership of the outcome. Over time, it can grow beyond protecting what was created and become more about continually refining it in the service of the client. Or as Kahlil Gibran puts it: "Work is love made visible."

For example, our team recently faced a difficult decision. In none of our previous builds had we ever sheathed our structures in plywood. Our unique framing method made it unnecessary. That was our big idea. But in Florida's high humidity, the plywood wrapping would preserve the home better over time. It meant adjusting a long-held standard. It meant sacrificing something I historically preferred and something that, until that point, had been a core idea behind our business.

We made the change to protect the client. And that, to me, is what invention as culture looks like.

To get there within your organization, here are some pointers learned over decades of entrepreneurship and service to the business, our people, and our clients. Think of these as a progression, not a checklist, each building on the one before it.

Redefine invention as a discipline. It is a repeated willingness to improve. For entrepreneurs, this matters because brilliance cannot scale, but discipline can. The common mistake is celebrating the breakthrough *without building the habits behind it.*

Anchor the work in gratitude. When you are grateful for the opportunity to serve, you do not cut corners. In construction, clients entrust us with possibly the largest investment of their lives. Forgetting that would breed complacency. Remembering it creates care.

Sacrifice preference for improvement. Let go of ego. The plywood decision in Florida is one example. We changed something that had worked for decades because it better served the client. The mistake is protecting tradition over outcome.

Choose a character before a skill. Skill is necessary but not sufficient. It is the character that determines whether the creative spirit survives beyond the founder. We have invested in partners and leaders not simply because they were talented, but because they cared deeply and could be trusted.

Design around a client's life. Every building is a new problem to solve. While the materials may be familiar, the lifestyle, the land, and the long-term function are unique. Companies lose their edge when they repeat themselves without listening.

And finally, institutionalize the culture.

When discipline, gratitude, sacrifice, character, and client focus are shared, the company no longer depends on one creative personality, moment, or breakthrough. Invention can embed itself. It can grow and become sustainable, enduring beyond its own conception.

There are practical business outcomes to all of this.

Geobarns is now led by a CEO who is not the founder, but this is not common. Many founder-led companies struggle to hand over leadership without losing their identity. When the creative force that built the business is gone, the edge softens. Our transition was only possible because the invention behind the business was never mine alone. It had already become shared practice, shared responsibility.

The company itself had become an invention built to endure.

Measuring What Matters

By Dawn Manske,
Founder, Dignity Alliance

Entrepreneurs often measure success through numbers that appear clean, precise, and objective. Revenue growth. Units sold. Customer acquisition. Profit margin. They matter, of course. A business that cannot sustain itself financially cannot accomplish much of anything.

But over time, I realized something important was missing from that conversation.

Success can look impressive on paper while depending on systems that undermine people along the way. A product can generate strong margins while the workers who produce it remain trapped in poverty. A brand can celebrate its social mission while contributing very little meaningful change. The numbers may look good, but the deeper story tells something else entirely.

That realization is part of what led me to establish Dignity Alliance, an umbrella framework that brings together the different parts of my work. Through Made for Freedom, our social enterprise provides employment opportunities for survivors of human trafficking. Through the nonprofit foundation, we support education and advocacy efforts that help communities better understand and respond to exploitation. Other initiatives connect people to these stories and encourage meaningful action.

The thread connecting all of it is dignity.

Over time, I have come to believe that dignity should be a core success metric, something leaders actively consider when deciding what success means for their business.

Most businesses focus on the middle of the transaction. What does it cost to make this product? What can we sell it for? What margin does that create?

These questions are not wrong, just incomplete.

When I talk about this with entrepreneurs, I often explain it simply: you have to think about what happens before the product comes in the door and after it goes out. The transaction in the middle is only part of the story.

In business terms, I often describe this as looking before the margin and after the margin.

If dignity is part of how you measure success, you have to look beyond the narrow slice of the transaction itself.

You have to look before the margin, at the supply chain that produced the product in the first place. Who made it? Under what conditions? Were they paid fairly? Did the work create opportunity, or did it perpetuate hardship? The cheapest option in a supply chain is often cheap for a reason.

To confuse this matter further, there is no price point that correlates with a lack of dignity. Without truly understanding the origin of a product, whether luxury design or bargain brands, problems persist within almost every industry.

You also have to look after the margin, at what the product represents once it reaches the customer. Does it simply disappear into a consumer cycle, or does it carry a story that helps people understand their connection to others? Does it create awareness, advocacy, and dignity beyond the moment of purchase?

These questions reshape how a business understands its role in the world.

One example comes from something as simple as a bracelet. At Made for Freedom, our bracelets represent employment for a survivor rebuilding her life. A portion of the sale supports education initiatives. And when someone asks about it, the person wearing the bracelet often shares the story behind it. In that moment, the product becomes advocacy.

A purchase becomes part of something larger.

The opposite is also true. Businesses sometimes tell powerful stories about doing good, while the deeper reality tells another story.

I experienced that firsthand when a friend's mother showed me a catalog of products claiming to support breast cancer research. I lost a friend to that disease, so the cause mattered deeply to me. I purchased a product from the catalog, assuming a meaningful portion of the purchase would go toward research.

Later, while looking more closely at the materials, I discovered that only 0.05 percent of each sale actually went to the cause.

Even more troubling, the catalog said nothing about where the product was made or under what conditions.

The experience clarified something important. A company can tell a compelling story about doing good while ignoring the dignity of the people who make its products.

When leaders measure success only by margin, those contradictions become easy to overlook.

Some popular business models highlight this tension. The "buy one, give one" approach captured enormous public attention. When a customer buys a product, the company donates a similar item to someone in need. The intentions were often genuine. In many cases, these models raised awareness and encouraged consumers to think about the impact of their purchases.

But they also reveal the limits of thinking only about impact after the margin. Providing free goods to communities does not always empower them. In some situations, it can unintentionally undermine local economies.

And if the products themselves are made in factories where workers are underpaid or working in unsafe conditions, then the good being done in one place may be offset by harm somewhere else.

That is why dignity has to become part of the success equation.

When entrepreneurs treat dignity as a metric, it reshapes their decisions in practical ways.

First, it encourages leaders to examine their supply chains honestly. Certifications like Fair Trade or B Corp can provide helpful guidance, but ultimately, dignity requires curiosity and responsibility.

Second, it encourages companies to close the gap between their story and their reality. When businesses market themselves as purpose-driven while their operations contradict that message, they undermine trust not only in their own brand but across entire sectors.

Finally, measuring dignity recognizes that consumers today are paying closer attention than ever before. People understand that their purchases have consequences, and they increasingly want to support brands that align with their values.

At its heart, entrepreneurship has always been about creating value. The real question is what kind of value we choose to measure.

If success is defined only by profit, businesses will naturally pursue the lowest costs and highest margins without considering who bears the hidden costs along the way.

But if dignity becomes part of the equation, the definition of success expands.

It asks leaders to look beyond what they earn in the middle of the transaction, to what their business costs before that moment, and what it creates afterward.

Because success is not only measured in the middle of the transaction. It is measured before the margin, in the dignity of the people who made the product. And it is measured after the margin, in the dignity it helps create in the world.

CHAPTER 25

Education as the Foundation of Entrepreneurship

By Carol Pfleiderer, HMCHA

I am not an entrepreneur. And yet, here I am, contributing to a book on entrepreneurship. Why?

I serve as the Sponsor Coordinator for the Holistic Ministry of Children of the Horn of Africa (HMCHA), working with children and families in rural Ethiopia. Long before, as a college student, I traveled to Brazil on a scholarship. What I imagined would be temporary became nearly seven years of teaching and living there, watching families navigate hardship. When I returned to the United States, I continued teaching. I have led dozens of Habitat for Humanity teams overseas and organized alternative gift fairs so families could support communities in need instead of exchanging more material things.

Over time, I began to understand something. Relief can ease suffering, but it is opportunity that changes direction.

When we first began sponsoring children in rural Ethiopia, high school was not even part of the conversation. Some parents had only completed a few years of school themselves. In certain village schools, children reached the middle grades without literacy skills. Expectations were small because exposure was small. If no one in your world has finished school, do you seriously consider going to college?

I don't want you to misunderstand what I'm saying. The barrier for these kids is not a lack of ambition, but access.

When our students began advancing in high school, challenges emerged. Sixteen-year-olds from remote villages were expected to move to a city, rent rooms, manage their time, cook, study, and navigate new and completely unfamiliar environments. For many, especially girls, it was overwhelming. So, we raised funds to purchase a home where students could live together with structure and shared responsibilities. We created space for study and mentorship.

What sticks with me still is how quickly dignity grows once opportunity appears. When a child can learn to read confidently, their posture changes, and when a student graduates from high school, their younger siblings begin to imagine new futures. When a young woman earns income, family dynamics shift.

In these contexts, education does more than increase earning potential; it restores agency. And agency, the ability to act in pursuit of a desired outcome, changes everything.

In many parts of the world, well-intentioned efforts focus primarily on giving: food, clothing, and short-term aid. In times of crisis, those acts are a lifeline. But if we stop there, we risk creating a cycle where needs return faster than solutions.

I have watched mothers form income-generating groups, save consistently, and plan together despite limited formal schooling. I have seen young people pursue higher education and return to their communities to help others with the skills they have gained. These shifts take time, and they happen through a steady investment in knowledge and confidence.

That shift, when it happens, is the birthplace of entrepreneurship. When people are equipped to solve problems themselves, when they can read contracts, manage finances, calculate risk, and make informed decisions, resilience grows, and opportunities once out of reach become attainable. They can begin small businesses, sell produce, raise livestock, or offer services within their own communities.

For business leaders, investors, and founders reading this, the lesson applies beyond rural Ethiopia. Many resilient enterprises begin in a similar way, with people who believe they are capable of something better. And for those who are yet to begin on their entrepreneurial path, learn to recognize the opportunities available, however limited they may seem. Understand that within you lies the very human ability to effect change, to improve your odds, and to move, step by step, in the direction of progress.

Whether that is for yourself, your business, your loved ones, your community or your country, the world will reward your persistence.

Realize that you are not merely a recipient of circumstance, but can also be a creator of value. Dignity, self-belief, agency: these things will not be handed to you. They grow when you recognize your own capabilities.

Education, whether that's from the classroom or the boardroom, nurtures that recognition. I began this journey because I cared about children. Along the way, I realized that education is one of the most strategic investments a society can make. It goes beyond preparing individuals for employment, providing the reinforcement necessary to create tomorrow's decision-makers, leaders, and yes, business owners.

Too often, people think of education as the phase before opportunity, when in reality it is the engine behind it. For entrepreneurs or those thinking of starting a business, understand that education never truly ends. The most successful people I've met are relentless learners. They read, adapt, seek mentors, analyze mistakes, and refine their thinking as their business grows. You will be required to question, to problem-solve, to imagine alternatives, and then make them real.

Whether creating a small business in Ethiopia or scaling a company in the US, progress belongs to those who commit to learning and then build something new with the opportunities that knowledge unlocks.

CHAPTER 26

Failure and Resilience Lead to Success

By James Webb,
Serial Entrepreneur and Author of
Redneck Resilience

My perspective on success and failure comes from experience, not theory. Over the course of my career, I have launched, acquired, and operated businesses across multiple industries, building and rebuilding ventures as markets shifted and opportunities evolved. I have seen both sides of entrepreneurship: the momentum of success and the reality of ventures that did not work out. Along the way, life has also delivered its share of personal loss and reinvention.

The way I think about resilience today comes from living through setbacks and learning that they are part of the process.

Entrepreneurship guarantees that things will go wrong at some point. The difference between the entrepreneurs who keep building and those who stop is not luck or timing. It is how they respond when the failure arrives.

One option is to quit. The other option is to stand back up and keep going. But standing back up does not mean charging forward blindly in the exact same direction.

Sometimes the smartest move is to change course.

That distinction is where resilience becomes real. We often say that entrepreneurs are determined, but let's admit it, entrepreneurs can be stubborn. It is absolutely crucial to recognize when an idea, product, or approach has reached its limits and adjust course before the next hit knocks you down again.

Many entrepreneurs struggle with this because they become attached to their original idea. There is even a term for it: marketing myopia. A founder can become so focused on proving the concept right that they stop paying attention to the signals around them. Instead of evaluating whether the product still works in the real world, they keep pushing simply because they can't imagine a world in which their idea fails.

I understand that instinct. Belief is necessary if you are going to build anything meaningful. But belief has to be balanced with reality. Some ideas deserve persistence. Others deserve a new direction.

That is one of the hardest skills an entrepreneur has to develop. Knowing when to push harder and when to pivot does not come from textbooks. It comes from experience. And very often, it comes from failure.

I tell people all the time that if you have not failed at least three times, you probably are not trying hard enough.

That line usually gets a laugh, but there is truth behind it. Success tends to reinforce what you already believe. Failure forces you to analyze what actually happened. It forces you to look at decisions, timing, capital, people, and strategy with a clearer lens. Those lessons are what shape better judgment.

I learned that lesson in 2003. I was dead broke and faced with a business decision that nobody around me wanted me to make. Every voice in the room pointed in one direction. My instincts pointed somewhere else.

I chose the direction nobody else wanted.

That single decision changed my life. Looking back, it was not simply the decision itself that mattered. It was the willingness to step away from the path everyone expected and move toward a different opportunity.

People often talk about gut instinct in entrepreneurship as if it were some mysterious talent. In reality, instinct is usually built from pattern recognition. When you spend enough time building companies, making deals, and solving problems, you begin to see patterns others might miss. Those patterns help you recognize when something is working and when it is time to pivot.

That does not mean entrepreneurs should operate in isolation. I am a strong believer in mentors. I believe in having people around you who have already walked the road you are traveling. I also believe in peers, and sometimes even competitors, as sources of insight. The ability to bounce ideas off people who understand the challenges of building a business can be incredibly valuable.

But there is a difference between listening and blindly following advice.

At some point, the entrepreneur has to make the call. You gather information. You weigh the options. And then you decide. Once the decision is made, you go.

Too many entrepreneurs hesitate after making a decision. They second-guess themselves. That hesitation does not stay contained in the founder's mind. It spreads into the organization. Teams feel it. Employees notice it. Leadership becomes weaker when conviction disappears.

A business needs someone willing to stand behind the direction and move forward with confidence. Without that, momentum disappears quickly.

Another hard reality many entrepreneurs face is capital. Many founders underestimate what it takes to build the infrastructure around an idea. Hiring the right people, building the right systems, and sustaining operations long enough for the business to stabilize requires resources.

That reality is why I often tell entrepreneurs to hope for the upside, but always plan for the downside.

Believing in the upside is essential. You cannot build a company without conviction and energy. But preparation matters just as much. When I evaluate a business opportunity, I absolutely focus on how it can succeed. At the same time, I ask another set of questions. What happens if this does not work? What happens if capital runs out? What happens if the market shifts?

If you have already considered the downside, you are less likely to be blindsided when problems arise. The goal is to ensure that failure does not catch you unprepared.

Entrepreneurship exists in an environment where uncertainty is constant. Disruptions appear from places nobody predicted. A global pandemic, supply chain breakdowns, or geopolitical events can suddenly change the landscape. You cannot anticipate every possible scenario, but you can build the habit of thinking ahead.

Resilience grows from that habit.

The entrepreneurs who build lasting success are not the ones who avoid failure entirely. They are the ones who absorb the lessons failure provides and apply them to the next venture. They remain ambitious, but they stay flexible. They listen, analyze, trust their judgment, and continue building.

CHAPTER 27

Capital Amplifies Character

By Freddy del Barrio,
Investor and Founder, Companion AI

Power reveals character. And capital simply amplifies whatever was already there.

Most entrepreneurs spend years focused on reaching the moment when they finally gain influence, scale, and resources. They imagine that success will change everything. Yet in reality, success mostly removes the barriers that once kept their instincts in check.

The habits they built when the company was small become the culture of the company when it is large. If those habits are grounded in humility and responsibility, growth strengthens the organization. And if they are rooted in ego, growth magnifies every weakness.

I have seen this play out repeatedly across industries, from hospitality to software to venture capital.

When a founder begins to experience traction, it becomes very easy to start believing your own mythology. Revenue is climbing. Investors are returning your calls. Teams are growing. At that point, the most dangerous thought an entrepreneur can have is the belief that past success proves permanent correctness. It doesn't. Markets evolve, technology changes, and new perspectives emerge constantly. The leaders who endure are the ones who remain open to hearing things they may not want to hear.

For me, that begins with the way teams are built. Founders often fall into the trap of surrounding themselves with people who reinforce their thinking. It feels efficient, even comfortable, to operate in a room where everyone agrees with you.

But comfort is not how companies evolve. The strongest organizations are built by people who approach problems from different vantage points. Experience matters. Youth matters. Technical depth matters. Cultural awareness matters.

When those perspectives meet in a room with mutual respect, ideas sharpen rather than stagnate.

In my own companies I have learned that age, background, and title matter far less than insight. A senior engineer who has spent decades building systems may see a risk that a founder overlooks. At the same time, someone early in their career may understand emerging consumer behavior in a way that a veteran leader does not. Both voices have value. If an organization only listens to one of them, it eventually loses the ability to adapt.

That openness also requires a founder to let go of something many entrepreneurs struggle with: control. Micromanagement is often mistaken for dedication, but it is usually a signal that something deeper is wrong. Either the wrong people have been hired, or the leader has not learned to trust them.

When a founder attempts to manage every detail of a growing company, two things happen simultaneously. The team loses confidence in its own ability to solve problems, and the founder burns out trying to carry a weight that should have been distributed.

Leadership is about creating an environment where capable people can solve problems together. When you hire the right individuals and give them the space to think, they often produce solutions more efficient than anything you could have designed alone. One of the greatest responsibilities of a founder is to recognize and create expertise throughout the organization, not just at the top.

This mindset becomes even more important when capital enters the picture.

Capital introduces scale, and scale introduces consequence. The decisions made by a founder with resources can shape industries, influence markets, and affect millions of people. That is why I believe investment should be treated as stewardship rather than spectacle. Deploying capital responsibly means asking whether the product or system being built truly improves lives.

Too much of the modern venture ecosystem is driven by hype cycles rather than durable solutions. Companies can achieve extraordinary valuations by capturing attention, collecting data, or chasing short-term adoption curves. But attention fades quickly. What lasts are systems that address real problems in the world. When entrepreneurs build with a genuine understanding of human need, the resulting companies tend to create both impact and sustainable growth.

That philosophy has guided my work with Companion AI. The idea emerged from a simple observation about the structure of modern healthcare. Clinical systems are designed around episodes of treatment: a hospital visit, a diagnosis, a procedure. Yet most of life happens outside those moments. Patients managing chronic conditions, seniors navigating aging, and veterans adjusting to civilian life often face long stretches of time without consistent support. The gap between clinical care and daily life is where isolation grows.

Technology alone cannot solve that problem, but it can help bridge it. The goal is to extend care, maintain context, and provide connection where traditional systems fall short. Building that kind of platform requires technical innovation, but it also requires an ethical commitment to the people who rely on it. Users are not just data points. They are individuals whose trust must be protected.

That belief extends to the broader responsibilities of entrepreneurship. The next generation of founders will operate in an environment where consumers, employees, and investors are increasingly aware of how companies behave. Questions about privacy, data use, and workplace culture are no longer secondary concerns. They are central to how organizations earn trust.

Entrepreneurs today have unprecedented access to capital, tools, and global markets. Those advantages create extraordinary opportunities, but they also demand a deeper sense of accountability. The real challenge is broader than simply building something profitable: it is building something worthy of the influence it will eventually hold.

Over time I have come to see success as a magnifier. It enlarges the intentions that drove the company from the beginning. If those intentions were rooted in ego, they eventually surface as dysfunction. If they were rooted in curiosity, integrity, and respect for others, they become the foundation of resilient organizations.

Every founder eventually reaches a moment when their influence grows beyond the early-stage hustle that started the journey. At that point, the question is no longer whether they can build a company. The question becomes what kind of company their character will produce.

Capital does not define that answer. It makes it visible.

CHAPTER 28

Make Epic Happen!

By Stephen Ritz,
Founder, Green Bronx Machine

People know me through the nonprofit I founded 15 years ago, Green Bronx Machine. I am known as a gardener or a farmer, and I grow vegetables in classrooms. What I really am, however, is an educator, social entrepreneur, and community builder. I grow people, schools, resilience, and opportunities. Plants are just the vehicle. Plus, they are nourishing, beautiful, translatable to cash, and capable of changing lives. I liken seeds to pennies, and when well planted, you have the equivalent of a $5 bill 30 days later.

At the core of my work is the belief that people should not have to leave their own neighborhood to live, learn, and earn in a better one. I believe that the greatest natural resource in the world is the undeveloped potential residing in low-status and marginalized communities. Coming from the South Bronx, I've lived and seen the inequities people write white papers about. I've watched systems fail children, families, and neighborhoods while pretending to offer solutions.

My goal is to end poverty in this lifetime by growing the next generation of independent young people. We cannot afford another generation of failed policy and ineffective, incremental nonprofit work. The stakes are too high, the planet is too toxic, and the reality is that we can end it. We just must want to do so collectively. And it will never happen without capitalism, social entrepreneurship, and virtuous, inclusive, and circular opportunities. Endless nonprofit work is not the answer.

The system isn't broken; it's doing exactly what it was designed to do: concentrate wealth and power into the hands of a few on the backs, hearts, lungs, minds, and wallets of as many as possible. We've created models that work best for those who claim to want to challenge the status quo, yet thrive due to its very nature. For far too long, I've seen people and organizations become fat and flush out communities like mine, pretending to be advocates for the solution. With each passing day, we see more nonprofits emerge, each claiming to be the solution we've been waiting for. Yet the problems get bigger and the solutions more elusive, requiring more money, donations, and time.

Simply put: you cannot nonprofit your way into prosperity. You can manage symptoms, you can build organizations that raise money around problems, and you can even create the appearance of progress. But if the goal is real transformation, if the goal is independence, affluence, and influence for the people you claim to serve, then you must build something very different. You must build ownership. You must build capacity. You must build systems that move people from being passive recipients of help to active producers of value.

Living, working, and teaching in my neighborhood taught me that the old model is upside down. We keep throwing money at problems and then acting surprised when the problems persist. But money alone does not create transformation. In many cases, it creates a false economy. It creates dependency. It creates an enterprise around the existence of the problem rather than a solution that makes the problem smaller. If your business model depends on the problem continuing, then you are not solving it. You are managing it.

I'm really interested in what happens when people begin to see themselves and their communities differently, when people realize they do not need someone else to save them, but that they themselves are the people they have been waiting for. It starts with three simple words: imagine, believe, act. Imagine means envisioning it and knowing what it looks like. Believing involves falling in love with that vision and prioritizing it above all. Act means committing yourself and your life to making it happen. For generations, I've seen this mindset succeed repeatedly in communities where people had been told to expect less.

For me, it starts with a very simple principle: move people from consumers to producers. In my world, that means taking children who have been told, directly or indirectly, that they are supposed to receive whatever the system hands them, and showing them that they can grow food, create value, solve problems, and contribute to and transform their communities. When a child grows food in a classroom, they are learning that they can create something real, something nourishing, something useful.

The same principle applies in entrepreneurship. If your customers, your employees, or your community only ever experience your business as a place where value is extracted from them, then you are building a fragile enterprise. But if your model allows people to participate, create, and rise with you, then you are building something durable. Ownership changes behavior. Stake changes expectations. When people feel they have a hand in the outcome, everything changes.

The second lesson is just as important: prioritize capacity over charity. I never ask for money first. I ask for capacity. I ask for tools, partnerships, infrastructure, access, distribution, visibility, and relevance. Lack of money can make you hungry, but capacity satisfies that appetite. Capacity is what allows people and organizations to do something repeatedly, measurably, and well. Charity may relieve the pressure for a moment, but capacity creates the possibility of lasting success.

The reason our work at Green Bronx Machine has been able to travel so far is because we built something replicable, teachable, and attractive to others. Today, the Green Bronx Machine curriculum is used in schools well beyond the Bronx because the model is not dependent on a single personality. It is dependent on systems that work. Entrepreneurs need to think the same way. If your business only functions when you are personally pushing every decision over the line, then you do not yet have a model. You have a hustle.

That leads to the third lesson: nail it before you scale it. Too many people confuse motion with progress. They want to expand before they have executed. They want to talk about impact before they have measured outcomes. They want to become known before they have become truly effective, or understood how to become better. I have always believed in execution over expansion. Under-promise and over-deliver. Know your outcome. Stay nimble. Learn quickly. Refine constantly.

The final lesson is the one that ties all the others together: think like an owner.

I tell people this all the time. I do not care whether you are a student, an educator, an employee, an entrepreneur, or an executive. Think like an owner. If you are not sitting at the table, you are probably being served on someone else's plate. Ownership is not just about equity or title. It is about responsibility. It is about acting as though your choices matter, because they do.

This is the mindset I want for young people. Not dependency. Not compliance. Not the quiet acceptance of predetermined limits. I want them to think huge, work together, solve problems, and see themselves as people who can create prosperity, not just hope somebody eventually shares it with them. Entrepreneurship, done right, teaches all these things.

I am often asked whether I really believe we can end poverty in this lifetime. I do. Absolutely. We live in a world of abundance. There are more people who are sick from what they're eating than there are who need food, and 40% of the food we grow is thrown away. Poverty is a distribution problem of both wealth and of opportunity. If we move people in poverty from bottom-end consumers into ongoing producers, they enter a virtuous cycle that elevates them out of poverty.

The issue is not scarcity. The issue is how wealth, opportunity, and power are structured and distributed. The issue is whether we have the courage to stop rewarding systems that preserve dysfunction and start investing in systems that produce dignity, health, agency, and prosperity. The future belongs to people who stop managing problems and start building systems that allow others to own solutions.

If you want to create something that lasts, do not build around dependency. Do not confuse activity with impact. Do not settle for managing the problem. Instead, move people from consumers to producers. Prioritize capacity over charity. Nail it before you scale it. And think like an owner.

From our humble corner of the globe, we are determined to change the world. You can too! Imagine, believe, act, and make epic happen!

Conclusion

Every entrepreneur in this collection has shown that success is not simply about having the right idea at the right time. It is about persistence, adaptation, and the courage to keep refining the vision until it becomes real. That is what makes these stories valuable: they do not romanticize the journey; they reveal it.

Taken together, these twenty-eight voices remind us that entrepreneurship is both practical and deeply human. It requires discipline, but also imagination. It demands structure, but also flexibility. Most of all, it asks for courage: to begin, to listen, to adjust, and to continue even when the outcome is uncertain.

That is the spirit *The Entrepreneurial Edge* captures so well. These are not just stories of business growth; they are stories of character, resilience, and meaningful contribution. They remind us that behind every brand is a person, and behind every person is a story worth telling.

May these pages leave you with more than inspiration. May they leave you with momentum. Because the real value of entrepreneurship is not only in what is built, but in who you become while building it.

Welcome to that future. Let's build it together.

— Omar Hamdi
Founder & CEO, Pathos Communications plc
London, 2026

Pathos Communications is a London-listed media technology company (LSE: NEWS) and the fastest-growing advertising/ marketing firm in Europe according to the Financial Times FT1000.